Chosen to Serve

Why Divine Election Is to Service, Not to Eternal Life

Chosen to Serve

Why Divine Election Is to Service, Not to Eternal Life

SHAWN LAZAR

Grace Evangelical Society
Denton, TX 76202

For Abby.

Contents

Take Off the Glasses

*"But isn't everything here green?" asked
Dorothy.*

*"No more than in any other city," replied
Oz; "but when you wear green spectacles,
why, of course, everything you see looks
green to you...My people have been wearing green glasses on their eyes for so long
that most of them think this really is an
Emerald City."*
THE WIZARD OF OZ[1]

"WHAT DO YOU MEAN you don't believe in
election?" I had been working for Bob at *Grace in
Focus* magazine for over a year. It was like being
in seminary again, only this time we were actually
studying the Bible. And I quickly learned that no

---

[1] L. Frank Baum, *The Complete Stories of Oz* (Hertfordshire: Wordsworth
Editions, 2012), 74.

9

doctrine was exempt from re-examination in light of God's Word. Bob had challenged me before. We debated all the time. But now I couldn't believe what I was hearing. No election?

"I didn't quite say that," Bob clarified. "What I said was, 'I don't believe in an election *to eternal life*.' I don't think the Bible teaches that."

"Of course it does," I protested. "Election is all over the Bible."

"Election *is* all over the Bible," Bob said. "But show me one verse that teaches God elects *individuals* to *everlasting life*."

"Well, there's got to be at least one verse that teaches it, even if it doesn't use that exact wording."

I went to my bookshelf and picked out my trusty copy of Steele, Thomas, and Quinn's *The Five Points of Calvinism* and flipped to the chapter on Unconditional Election.[2] "Here's what they write," I said. "'There are general statements in Scripture that God has an elect people, and that He predestined them to salvation, and thus to eternal life.'"

"OK. They say God chooses people to eternal life. And by *people* they mean *individuals*, right? So, what verses do they use?"

"The first one is from Deut 10:14-15: 'Behold, to the Lord your God belong heaven and the

---

2 David N. Steele, Curtis C. Thomas, S. Lance Quinn, *The Five Points of Calvinism: Defined, Defended, and Documented*, Second Edition (Phillipsburg, NJ: P&R Publishing, 2004), 29.

heaven of heavens, the earth with all that is in it. Yet the Lord set his heart in love on your fathers and chose their offspring after them, you above all peoples, as you are this day."

"Stop right there," Bob said. "Notice anything missing?"

"No. What?"

"They said these verses teach that God elects people to eternal life, right? Well, where does that verse say that?"

"It says that God loved and chose their fathers and their offspring."

"Whose fathers? Whose offspring?"

"The Jews."

"Do all the Jews have eternal life?"

"No."

"So God lovingly choosing someone doesn't automatically mean he gets eternal life?"

"Well, I don't know about that. It's individuals within the Jewish people that He loves."

"Does this verse say that? Does it say God's love or choice is limited to a few Jews?" Bob asked. "Are any individuals even mentioned here at all?"

"No," I admitted.

"What about eternal life? Does it mention that?"

I read the verses again. "No. But God elects them *for something.*"

"Exactly, but for what?" Bob was getting excited. "That's the whole question. All I see is

a general comment about God's choosing the
Jews as a group. But there's no explanation about
what they were chosen for. There's no mention
of individuals. There's certainly no mention of
predestination. And there's no mention of eternal
life. So why would they quote that verse to show
God predestines individuals to eternal life when it
doesn't say that at all?"

He had a point.

"Fine, I'll grant you that one," I said. "But
here's a quote from Ps 33:12: 'Blessed is the nation
whose God is the Lord, the people whom He has
chosen as His heritage!'"

"Same problem as before," Bob pointed out. "It
says God chose the Jewish nation. That is a general statement about God's corporate election of
Israel. I accept that. I believe in corporate election.
But for what purpose? The authors are talking
about individual predestination to eternal life.
Where does the verse teach that? There's no mention of individuals or of eternal salvation."

"Well, hold your horses, now, they quote a few
more verses."

So we read them together. And as we did, a
pattern began to emerge. The authors would quote
a verse involving a divine choice, but there was no
clear mention of individuals or of eternal salvation. I was getting puzzled. Why would they quote
those verses to prove unconditional election to
eternal life?

Simply put, they did what we all tend to do: *They read their beliefs into the Bible.*

The authors were like Dorothy wearing tinted glasses that made everything look green in the Emerald City. Except, in this case, their glasses made every reference to election look like it taught individual election to eternal life.

For example, they quoted Ps 106:5 which actually says,

> ...that I may look upon the prosperity of your chosen ones, that I may rejoice in the gladness of your nation, that I may glory with your inheritance.

In their minds, they saw the words "chosen ones" and assumed it meant something like,

> ...that I may look upon the prosperity of [*the individuals you have predestined to eternal life*], that I may rejoice in the gladness of your nation, that I may glory with your inheritance.

I hope you agree, that's a sloppy way of interpreting the Bible.

Of course, if we're being honest, we all make the same mistake, don't we? We all wear tinted glasses sometimes. I know I do. In fact, up until that moment, I think Steele and I shopped at the same store!

As Bob and I went through the rest of the verses together, he had clear interpretations for most of them showing they were not about individual predestination to eternal life. But, admittedly, there were a handful of verses that he couldn't explain off the top of his head to either of our satisfaction.

"I tell you what," Bob said. "Do some research. I want an article on this. I'm willing to believe in an election to eternal life, *if* that's what the Bible teaches. In fact, I used to believe that. But I have a feeling we've been missing what the Bible actually says about election."

So I hit the books. Again. I've read much of the classic literature on election, but I was wearing tinted glasses. Now I re-read those books—including the Bible—trying to keep those assumptions in check. And I soon came to a surprising conclusion: *There isn't a single verse in the entire Bible that speaks about God's electing individuals to eternal life.*

Not a one.

Not one!

A few verses come *close*, or at least *seem* to if you're already committed to the idea of predestination to salvation.

As brilliant as much of the election literature has been, I think it has mostly been driven by confessional commitments. What I mean is, election debates have been going on for centuries, and over time, denominations have adopted official positions on the subject, wrote them into their official confessions, and expected their seminarians, pastors, and theologians to defend those positions.

Peoples' jobs were on the line. How did Upton Sinclair put it? "It is difficult to get a man to understand something, when his salary depends on his not understanding it."

Of course, it's only natural for people to want to defend the churches and denominations they love. I understand that. I applaud that. It's a noble instinct. We should love our churches.

But when your church or denomination has an official position on election that you are expected to believe and defend, that creates a lot of pressure to follow the party line instead of finding out the truth for yourself. It makes it hard for people to study the Bible with a fresh pair of eyes.

And that's what I'd like to do here, with you.

Let's start over.

Let's pretend we have no idea what the Bible teaches about election and build our understanding from the ground up.

We'll do a series of word studies on the key terms in the election debate, but instead of concentrating on only a handful of verses about election, we'll survey how election is portrayed *throughout the Bible*.

Only after we've done an overview of the Bible's big picture about election will we take a closer look at the classic verses that are most often used to support individual election to eternal life.

Here is my challenge to you. Regardless of what you already believe about election, I invite you to treat this book *as a hypothesis.*

This isn't a polemic or an attack.

It's a thought experiment.

As someone who was once thoroughly convinced of predestination to eternal life, I know how hard it is to read the Bible any other way.

But it *is* possible.

This book shows you how and why my mind was changed one verse at a time. Maybe yours will be, too.

Human Election in the Old Testament

Choose well. Your choice is brief, and yet endless.

JOHANN WOLFGANG VON GOETHE

1. Introduction

ONE OF THE HARDEST things about growing up in Montreal was trying to find a wife. The problem wasn't a lack of girls. The problem was my faith. I was an Evangelical in a deeply secular city. There were only a few thousand Evangelicals in the whole province of Quebec. So once I narrowed it down to Christian girls who were English-speaking, my age, and single, and after dating both of them, what could I do?

I definitely didn't want to date an unbeliever.

We used to call that "missionary dating." What I quickly realized is that missionary dating works both ways. The Christian might be subtly sharing his faith with his girlfriend, but she was doing the same with him. I had seen it tried many times and the results were always the same: the Christian would fall away from the faith.

Every. Single. Time.

No wonder God warned Israel: "You must not marry them [the Gentiles], because they will turn your hearts to their gods" (1 Kgs 11:2a NLT).

That's what happened to King Solomon. He had hundreds of pagan wives, and his faith didn't stand a chance. Before too long the world's wisest man became an idolater:

> For when Solomon was old, his wives
> turned his heart away after other gods;
> and his heart was not wholly devoted to
> the Lord his God, as the heart of David his
> father had been (1 Kgs 11:4).

If the wisest man in the world was led to idolatry by his heathen wives, would I do any better? Probably not. And I'm glad I didn't try. In my last year of college I discovered the world's most beautiful redhead lived in Texas, and by some miracle, I convinced her to marry me.

My point is, marriage is one of the most important choices you'll ever make. So choose wisely!

That is what Biblical election is about: choices.

Thousands of pages have been written defending the idea that God chooses individuals to have eternal life, so you would expect to find that doctrine taught throughout the OT.

But it's not.

Yes, *election* itself is mentioned many times, but election *to what*?

Although the standard works on election place all the focus on God's choices, a truly Biblical understanding of election will take in all the evidence, including those OT examples in which *people* do the electing. That's what we'll look at in this chapter.

2. What Do the Words Mean?

In English, the word *election* has to do with a choice. To *elect* something or someone means *to choose* it or him. And whatever we choose becomes elect.

Think of politics. During an election different candidates make their case for why they should hold office. We choose a candidate and vote for him. If he gets enough votes, he gets elected.

The Hebrew and Greek words for election are very close to the common English meaning.

The primary Hebrew word for election is *bachār*. It means "to choose, select, elect, decide for, or prefer,"[1] and it occurs 172 times in 164 verses.[2] In turn, *bachār* has several derivatives, including *chosen* (*bachir*), *choicest/best* (*mibhār*), and *choice* (*mibhir*).

Here is how the *Theological Dictionary of the Old Testament* defines the word:

> The Hebrew root *bhr* means a careful choice occasioned by actual needs, and thus a very conscious choice and one that can be examined in light of certain criteria, in contrast perhaps to making a selection, to deciding as an act of an especially intimate relationship, or to "taking" (*laqach*) and "determining" (*ho'il*).[3]

The dictionary goes on to explain that,

> Everywhere that *bhr* occurs in relationship to persons, it denotes choice out of a group (generally out of the totality of the

---

[1] R. Laird Harris, Gleason L. Archer, Jr., Bruce K. Waltke, *Theological Workbook of the Old Testament* (Chicago, IL: Moody, 1980), 100; *Mounce's Complete Expository Dictionary of Old & New Testament Words*, eds. William D. Mounce, D. Matthew Smith, Miles Van Pelt (Grand Rapids, MI: Zondervan, 2006), 107.

[2] A. Philip Brown, II. "Election in the Old Testament." See http://evangelicalarminians.org/wp-content/uploads/2013/04/Brown.-Election-in-the-Old-Testament.pdf. Accessed October 21, 2013.

[3] *Theological Dictionary of the Old Testament*, eds. G. Johannes Botterwck and Helmen Ringgren, trans. John T Willis (Grand Rapids, MI: Eerdmans, 1983), 2:74.

people), so that the chosen discharges a function in relationship to the group.[4]

So the word *bachār* means *to choose*. But this isn't just any old choice. It is a careful and practical choice that best meets the needs at hand.

We can't review every single mention of human election or choice in the OT. That would make for a very long book. But if you look over the various uses, you'll see they tend to fall into distinct categories. Getting a handle on those categories will give us a good overview of how the OT presents election.

3. Categorizing the Biblical Evidence

A. People, Places, and Things

(i) Wives

Someone once quipped, "What woman doesn't believe her husband had better taste in choosing a partner than she did?"

We may not think of marriage as a type of election, but Biblically speaking it is. I chose my wife. She chose me. We were both elect in each other's eyes. Just so, the OT is full of examples of men *choosing* wives for themselves.

---

[4] Ibid., 2:82-83.

…that the sons of God saw that the daughters of men were beautiful; and they took wives for themselves, *whomever they chose* (Gen 6:2, emphasis added).

(ii) Places to Live

After figuring out whom to marry, one of the biggest choices we can make is where to live, a conversation my wife and I have spent long hours discussing. Where should we live, we wondered? Canada? The US? Europe? I've got a travelling bug. All the Lazar men do. My great-great-grand-father moved from Germany to modern-day Croatia. My great-grandfather moved from Croatia to England. His son, my father, moved from England to Canada. I moved from Canada to the U.S. Who knows where my son will end up? We're wanderers.

Abraham was a wanderer, too. He went from Ur to Canaan and pitched his tent between Bethel and Ai, only to move to Egypt when famine struck, and then moved again after Pharaoh kicked him out.

Along the way, Abraham got rich. So did his nephew Lot. You'd think they'd be happy. But as Benjamin Franklin once said, money doesn't *fill* a vacuum; it *creates* one.

The Bible says that Abraham and Lot had so many possessions it created tension between them: "And the land could not sustain them while dwelling together, for their possessions were so great that they were not able to remain together" (Gen 13:6).

The land was crowded and resources were scarce. The herdsmen began fighting over water and grazing rights for their animals. They couldn't live in peace together, so they decided to go their own way. Abraham asked Lot to pick any part of the land and move there.

> So Lot *chose* for himself all the valley of the Jordan, and Lot journeyed eastward. Thus they separated from each other (Gen 13:11, emphasis added).

Lot looked and saw that Jordan was full of water—clear, cool, bubbling water—with green grass and gentle terrain. It was perfect for livestock, and suited his purposes, so Lot chose it. He elected it. And he left.

(iii) Sacrificial Animals

Do you remember Elijah's famous challenge to the four hundred and fifty prophets of Baal?

Israel was slipping away from the Lord. People were going after idols. Elijah knew they needed a sign to come back to the true faith. So he challenged the opposition to a duel. Elijah instructed the prophets of Baal to choose two bulls, one prepared by them and the other prepared by him. Whichever god sent fire to consume the sacrifice would be worshipped as the true God.

The prophets accepted Elijah's challenge and *chose* the bulls:

> "Now let them give us two oxen; *and let them choose one ox* for themselves and cut it up, and place it on the wood, but put no fire under it; and I will prepare the other ox and lay it on the wood, and I will not put a fire under it" (1 Kgs 18:23, emphasis added).

(iv) People, Places, and Things

So far we've looked at three example of Biblical election: marriage, places to live, and sacrificial animals.

You will notice that choices are not necessarily about human beings. You can elect an animal for a sacrifice.

You will also notice that it isn't always about individuals, since a piece of land can be elect.

You will also notice these were all choices in time. Election is often presented as something that happens beyond time and space. But not here. People, places, and things are chosen in the moment to serve that moment's needs.

And lastly, you'll notice that all of these choices were *vocational*. That is, they were for some kind of service or occupation. A woman was chosen to serve as a wife. The piece of land was chosen to serve as a home. The bulls were chosen to serve as a sacrifice. People, places, and things were all chosen to serve a particular function or purpose.

So far, we haven't seen an election to eternal life. But it's still early yet.

B. Choosing to Serve God

Bob Dylan sang, "You're gonna have to serve somebody; it may be the devil or it may be the Lord. But you're gonna have to serve somebody."

Everyone has to serve someone, but not every type of service is equally fulfilling, or profitable, or godly. Some people spend their whole lives searching for the things that will only destroy them in the end. As Jesus asked, "What will it profit a man if he gains the whole world, and loses his own soul?" (Mark 8:36).

Given the choice between God and the world, between serving the wicked in a glamorous position or serving the Lord in a menial one, the Psalmist's answer is clear:

> For a day in Your courts is better than a thousand outside. *I would rather stand at the threshold* of the house of my God than dwell in the tents of wickedness (Ps 84:10, emphasis added).

Once again, we see the vocational nature of election. This is a choice for service.

Unsurprisingly, the idea of choosing to serve the Lord is found in many other verses. For example,

Joshua urged the tribes of Israel to choose to follow
God instead of the neighboring pagan deities:

> "If it is disagreeable in your sight to serve
> the Lord, *choose for yourselves today whom*
> *you will serve*: whether the gods which
> your fathers served which were beyond
> the River, or the gods of the Amorites in
> whose land you are living; but as for me
> and my house, we will serve the Lord"
> (Josh 24:15, emphasis added; cf. Deut
> 30:19).

Although this choice was deeply religious, it
was also vocational. It had to do with religious
service. Would the Hebrews worship the gods of
Egypt or the gods of the Amorites, or would they
serve the Lord? Joshua and his house chose the
Lord. Not everyone is as wise (cf. Isa 66:3). What
have you and your family chosen?

Isaiah complained that Israel had forsaken the
Lord. Instead of choosing the way of faithfulness
(Ps 119:30, 173) they chose to associate with the
trees and gardens of idolatry (Isa 1:29).

God calls you and me to choose faithfulness.
Choose Him. He has spoken His Word, given His
commands, issued His promises. Will you and
your family believe? Or will you serve the gods of
this world?

These verses show there is a sense in which *we*
elect ourselves. We choose to be faithful or not. We

choose whom or what to worship. And we choose whom or what to serve. We can choose to align ourselves with God or walk away from Him.

C. Choice as a Quality

One of my Saturday rituals is going to the farmer's market to pick out fresh vegetables. If I've learned anything about cooking over the years, it's that your dishes are only as good as your ingredients. For example, I used to eat store bought guacamole. Then one day I tried making it from scratch. There is no comparison! Packaged guacamole simply cannot compete with fresh avocados, onions, jalapenos, lime, tender cilantro, and just a hint of salt.

Fresh is better, every time.

If you haven't tried it, I would urge you to give it a shot. (Start off by mashing the avocado until it is creamy, then add the other ingredients.)

At the farmer's market, my daughter and I carefully pick out each fruit and vegetable. We're careful of what we buy because we don't want to waste money on a rotten piece of fruit. We're paying good money, and we want quality.

Did you know that chosenness can also be about a *quality*?

We're all familiar with that language, aren't we? We speak about "select" cuts of meat at a butcher or "choice" seats at a concert in order to convey their special quality.

The OT uses the same terminology. People are called "chosen" or "choice" because they have outstanding characteristics that make them best suited for an important mission.

(i) King Saul

For example, when Israel was choosing its first king, the popular vote went to Saul because he was taller and more handsome than the other candidates. He *looked* like a king. Here's how he was described:

> He had a son whose name was Saul, *a choice* and handsome man, and there was not a more handsome person than he among the sons of Israel; from his shoulders and up he was taller than any of the people (1 Sam 9:2, emphasis added).

(ii) Elite Soldiers

Or consider how, when certain soldiers were chosen to undertake a mission, they were sometimes called "choice" men. Why? Because they were especially fit for the task at hand.

The use of "choice" as a quality was often used in a military setting. I've heard it said the object of war is not to die for your country but to *make the other guy* die for his. Hence, when it came to going to war, kings paid careful attention to who would do the fighting.

Here are some examples of men called *choice* in a *qualitative* sense:

> David again assembled all *the choice men* in Israel, 30,000 (2 Sam 6:1, HCSB, emphasis added).

> From the cities on that day the sons of Benjamin were numbered, 26,000 men who draw the sword, besides the inhabitants of Gibeah who were numbered, 700 choice men. Out of all these people 700 *choice men* were left-handed; each one could sling a stone at a hair and not miss (Judg 20:15-16, emphasis added).

There are many other verses where *chosen* or *choice* are used in a qualitative sense (cf. Exod 14:7; 1 Sam 24:2; 1 Chron 19:10; 2 Chron 13:3, etc). Keep that in mind, because it will play an important role in the NT, which also uses *choice* in a qualitative sense.

4. Conclusion

In this chapter, we've already covered a lot of ground and we're just getting started. What does the evidence suggest so far?

It suggests that election is down-to-earth and practical. When the OT uses *election*, people, places, and things *are chosen to serve a purpose.* In other words, election is *vocational.*

That is true even when election has a qualitative meaning. Someone (or something) is considered *choice* because he possess qualities that make him suitable *for the job.*

Now, I'm sure some of you are probably thinking that all this talk of human choices, while vaguely fascinating, is really beside the point. You might think the heart of the Biblical doctrine of election is about *divine* choices, not human ones. When *humans* do the choosing, it may be all mundane and down-to-earth, but when it's *God* doing the electing it becomes the deeply mysterious and philosophical doctrine that seminary students love fighting over well into the night.

Is that right?

Does the Bible portray God's choices completely differently from human ones?

Let's find out in the next chapter.

2

Divine Choices in the Old Testament

*God chooses the most unlikely candidates
to fulfill his purposes.*
JOHN SAWARD[1]

1. Introduction

MILES DAVIS WAS ONE of the greatest jazz musicians of all time. That isn't to say he was a virtuoso trumpet player. The truth is there were better trumpeters out there. For example, Davis didn't have Dizzy Gillespie's chops or range. He had technical deficiencies and made mistakes. Listen carefully to his albums, and you'll hear them.

But even though there were better players, few could rival Davis musically. Why not?

---

[1] John Saward, *Perfect Fools: Folly for Christ's Sake in Catholic and Orthodox Spirituality* (New York, NY: Oxford University Press, 1980, 2000), 3.

Davis was aware of his weaknesses and used them to his advantage. He didn't try to fit as many notes and scales as he could into a song. He chose his notes carefully. He played off the silences. He made every note count. Even his mistakes seemed intentional.

But even more importantly, Davis was a great bandleader.

As pianist Chick Corea once noted,

> "Miles always had this wonderful characteristic of gravitating toward a creative musician and then having the intelligence to know how to utilize that musician within his own sphere without cramping the guy's style."[2]

Part of Davis's genius was that he always surrounded himself with the very best players in the world. He chose musicians who enhanced his own playing and who could bring his musical vision to life. And over the course of his career, Davis reinvented jazz several times over.

Whether notes or bandmates, Davis knew how to choose wisely.

Likewise, everyone agrees that God chooses. Divine election is written across the pages of the

---

[2] See http://www.today.com/id/33196293/ns/today-today_entertainment/t/miles-davis-masterly-kind-blue-turns/#.VCNprildXs4. Accessed July 10, 2015.

OT. The question is, why does He choose? What are those choices about? What is divine election?

In the last chapter we saw that human election was quite ordinary. People, places, and things were chosen to serve human purposes. Human election was earthy and vocational.

Is divine election any different? Are God's choices as mysterious as theologians and philosophers make them out to be?

Let's survey some of the evidence.

2. God Chose Moses

When the Hebrews lived as slaves in Egypt, they prayed for a deliverer. God sent Moses.

A. God Chose a Deliverer

We're all familiar with Moses' story. As the Bible tells us, Moses was born a Hebrew, raised as a prince of Egypt, fled to the wilderness, returned to Egypt as an old man, demanded that Pharaoh let his people go, and then led the Hebrews out of Egypt, across the Red Sea.

Suffice it to say, Moses understood that he was chosen by God. But why? For eternal life? No. To accomplish an important mission:

> Moses said, "By this you shall know that the LORD has sent me *to do all these*

deeds; for this is not my doing" (Num
16:28, emphasis added).

God sent Moses to do works, i.e., to lead the
Jews out of Egypt into the Promised Land.

This was not an election to eternal life. Moses
was chosen to serve.

B. God Did Not Choose the Rebels

Once in the wilderness, the Jews began to
complain against Moses. Egypt and Israel are
neighbors. It's a seven hour drive from Cairo to
Jerusalem. It would take about eight days of walk-
ing. But the Hebrews were in the wilderness *for
years*!

No wonder the people complained. Can you
blame them? But some took it too far.

Three men named Korah, Dathan, and Abiram
even rebelled against Moses and challenged his
leadership. So Moses called on God to show who
was truly elected to lead the people:

> …and he spoke to Korah and all his
> company, saying, "Tomorrow morning
> the Lord will show who is His, and who is
> holy, and will bring him near to Himself;
> even the one *whom He will choose*, He will
> bring near to Himself (Num 16:5, empha-
> sis added).

God gave a very decisive answer:

Now it came to pass, as he finished speaking all these words, that the ground split apart under them, and the earth opened its mouth and swallowed them up, with their households and all the men with Korah, with all their goods. So they and all those with them went down alive into the pit; the earth closed over them, and *they perished from among the assembly* (Num 16:31-33, emphasis added).

God made it very clear that if you aren't fulfilling your calling, you could be cut off from the assembly by an early death (cf. Gen 17:14; Exod 12:15; 30:33; Lev 23:29; Num 9:13). That's what happened to Korah and his men. They rebelled against Moses and rejected his divine election, thereby repudiating their own election by God to serve as members of the chosen people. As a result, God punished them with physical death.

C. Moses Failed

But, before you judge Korah and his men too harshly, remember that Moses failed, too. God had told him to *speak* to a rock and water would gush forth. Instead, Moses *struck* the rock. God revealed this showed a lack of faith and reverence. Consequently, Moses was denied entry to the Promised Land:

Then Moses lifted up his hand and struck
the rock twice with his rod; and water
came forth abundantly, and the congrega-
tion and their beasts drank. But the Lord
said to Moses and Aaron, "Because you
have not believed Me, to treat Me as holy
in the sight of the sons of Israel, therefore
you shall not bring this assembly into
the land which I have given them" (Num
20:12).

Moses never completed his vocation. He was
chosen to lead the people into the Promised Land.
Instead, he only got to bring them near it, and
died outside.

To be clear, the fact that Moses was punished
with an early death does not mean that he went
to hell, or wasn't really saved, or lost his salvation.
Moses died physically, but that doesn't mean he
also died spiritually. Eternal life or death is not in
view here.

Moses' election was vocational, not eternal.
He had a job to do in this life, and when he failed,
God punished him with temporal death.

3. God Chose Jeremiah

In a passage that is typical of many of the great
prophetic figures in the OT, we are told that God
chose Jeremiah to be a prophet,

> "*I chose you* before I formed you in the womb; I set you apart before you were born. I appointed you a prophet to the nations" (Jer 1:5 HCSB, emphasis added).

Many translations have "I knew you" instead of "I chose you." That is because the Hebrew word *yada* (to know) can have elective significance when it is combined with other terms, as it is here.[3]

God knew Jeremiah, and *set him apart* and *appointed* him to be a prophet. And why did God know or choose Jeremiah? For eternal life? No. As the text says, he was chosen before conception to serve as a prophet to Israel. Jeremiah's election was vocational.

4. The Servant of Yahweh

The OT also teaches us about the election of the Suffering Servant (Isa 49:7). The fact that he was anointed by God (Isa 61:1) signified His election. But why was He chosen?

As His very title suggests, the Servant was chosen *to serve*. That's what servants do.

What was the Suffering Servant chosen to do? To bring Jacob and Israel back to God (49:5), to restore the preserved remnant of Israel (49:6),

---

[3] William W. Klein, *The New Chosen People: A Corporate View of Election* (Grand Rapids, MI: Zondervan, 1990), 31.

to be a light to the Gentiles (49:6), to restore the earth (49:8), and to set the captives free (49:9). And perhaps most important of all, the Servant was chosen to suffer for man's salvation (Isa 52:13—53:12).

The Suffering Servant's election was thoroughly vocational.

And if there's any doubt about that point, consider this: we know the Suffering Servant is the Messiah, Jesus Christ. And we know that Jesus Christ was definitely not elected to eternal life, because He is the Source of that life!

5. God Elects Places

God not only elected *individuals* to serve Him, He also elected *cities*. The most obvious example would be the election of Jerusalem:

> "When Your people go out to battle against their enemy, wherever You send them, and when they pray to the Lord toward *the city which You have chosen* and the temple which I have built for Your name" (1 Kgs 8:44, emphasis added; cf. 8:48; 11:13, 32, 36; 14:21; 2 Kgs 21:7; 23:27; 2 Chron 6:6, 34, 38; 12:13; 33:7; Neh 1:9; Ps 132:13; Zech 3:2).

As a sign of Jerusalem's election, God had the Temple built there, which, by the way, is another example of a place that was elected by God,

> "For now *I have chosen and sanctified this house*, that My name may be there forever; and My eyes and My heart will be there perpetually" (2 Chron 7:16, emphasis added; cf. 33:7).

Jerusalem was elect, the Temple was elect, and so was Mt Zion, the hill upon which the Temple was built:

> For *the Lord has chosen Zion*; He has desired it for His dwelling place (Ps 132:13, emphasis added; cf. 78:68).

Three places chosen by God. None were chosen for eternal life, but to serve His purposes.

And they were not the only places God elected. Many other places were chosen to serve His purposes (e.g., Deut 12:5, 11, 14, 18, 21, 26; 14:23, 25; 15:20; 16:2, 7, 11, 15, 16; 17:8, 10; 18:6; 26:2; 31:11. Cf. also Josh 9:27; 2 Chron 7:12).

Clearly, these are vocational elections. And as we saw with other vocational elections, they were conditional.

For example, if the people of Jerusalem or the Temple didn't serve God's purposes, they would suffer the consequences.

Due to Israel's apostasy, the Babylonians destroyed Jerusalem in 586 BC (Jeremiah 52, Lam 1:8-9), and the Romans destroyed it in AD 70 (see the Lord's warning in Luke 13:2-5, 34-35). Likewise, the Temple was sacked and destroyed twice times.

Nevertheless, both Jerusalem and the Temple will serve again once the Messiah comes back to restore the kingdom to Israel (Acts 1:6).

6. Conclusion

When God elects, He chooses people, places, and things to serve Him. Thus far, OT election is thoroughly *vocational*. You should also have noticed that election is also *conditional*. There was no guarantee of success. If an elect person failed in his mission, he could be punished, up to and including being killed or destroyed.

So far the evidence doesn't quite fit the traditional picture of election as a timelessly eternal choice of individuals for heaven or hell. But it is still early in our study.

3

The Individual/Corporate Pattern

All for one, and one for all.
THE THREE MUSKETEERS

1. Introduction

MY GREAT-GRANDMOTHER, Katerina Staub, was Yugoslavian. Her second husband, Alexander Saganenko, was Russian. I remember their apartment in Montreal being filled with mementos from the old country.

On one shelf she had a matryoshka doll, better known as a Russian nesting doll. I'm sure you've seen them before. The doll was shaped like a big wooden egg painted to resemble a babushka, an Orthodox woman wearing a head covering. If you unscrewed the top of the doll, you would find another, smaller doll inside it. And if you unscrewed the top of that one, you'd find an even smaller

41

doll. When all was said and done you'd have a set of at least five dolls from small to big.

As silly as it sounds, those dolls have something to teach us about divine election.

We know that God can choose an individual for a mission. But the Bible also tells us those individual choices are often *implicitly corporate*. In other words, when God chose an *individual* to serve Him, He was often implicitly choosing *a group of people* to continue the same mission. I call it the individual/corporate pattern in election, and we'll explore it further in this chapter.

2. Abraham and the Jews

The most obvious place to begin studying the individual/corporate pattern of divine election is in the ancient city of Ur.

A. God Chose Abraham

Ur was located in modern-day Iraq. It was a Sumerian city-state. And four thousand years ago, God met with a man named Abram (who was later renamed Abraham) and made him an extraordinary promise.

We aren't specifically told that Abram was *chosen* or *elect*, but he clearly was.

Moreover, God chose Abram for a special purpose:

> Now the Lord had said to Abram:
> "Get out of your country,
> From your family
> And from your father's house,
> *To a land that I will show you.*
> *I will make you a great nation*;
> I will bless you
> And make your name great;
> And you shall be a blessing.
> I will bless those who bless you,
> And I will curse him who curses you;
> *And in you all the families of the earth shall*
> *be blessed"* (Gen 12:1-3 NKJV, emphasis added).

God had a mission for Abram. He told him to leave his country in order to start a new one. God promised to give Abram a land that he could populate, so he could become a great nation, and be a blessing to all the families of the earth.

Even though the usual words associated with election are not found here, no one would disagree that God elected Abram.

Moreover, I trust that you can see that Abram's election was vocational. He had a mission to accomplish. He was called to be a settler, a father, and a founder. He was chosen to serve.

B. *Through Abraham, God Chose the Jews*

When God chose Abram as an individual, his election was implicitly corporate. When God chose Abram, He already had a people in mind. In fact, God changed Abram's name to Abraham which means *the father of many nations* because Abraham would become the forebear to a new people, the Jews.

Indeed, by far the most frequent use of the concept of election is in reference to the Jews, and if you want to understand OT election you need to understand how and why the Jews are God's chosen people:

> "For you are a holy people to the Lord your God; the Lord your God *has chosen you to be a people* for His own possession out of all the peoples who are on the face of the earth" (Deut 7:6, emphasis added; cf 14:2).

> "But now listen, O Jacob, My servant, and Israel, *whom I have chosen*" (Isa 44:1, emphasis added).

> Blessed is the nation whose God is the Lord, *the people whom He has chosen* for His own inheritance (Ps 33:12, emphasis added).

Israel's election was not arbitrary. God was moved to choose the Jews out of love for them:

> "Because He loved your fathers, therefore *He chose their descendants* after them" (Deut 4:37a, emphasis added; cf. Deut 7:7-8; 10:15).

Given all these verses, no one can doubt the Jews are the quintessential "chosen people." But consider this astonishing fact: despite numerous mentions of the Jews being chosen by God *there isn't a single reference to the Jews's being chosen for eternal life.* Not one. That idea is absent from the OT. So why were the Jews elected if it wasn't to have eternal life?

C. Israel Was Chosen to Be a Nation of Priests

> "And you shall be to Me *a kingdom of priests* and a holy nation" (Exod 19:6a, emphasis added).

Israel was chosen by God for a mission: to serve as a nation of priests. Their vocation was to worship and serve the Lord: offering Him praise, glorifying His name, and attending to His presence.

Crucially, Israel was meant to serve as priests on behalf of the Gentile world (Rom 2:17-20), living according to God's Law and teaching the Gentiles to do the same.

In that respect, Israel's election was unique. No other nation was chosen for that purpose.

And note that this was entirely vocational. Israel was not chosen to have eternal life.

D. Individual Jews Were Conditionally Elect

God chose Israel as a group, but nowhere did God guarantee that every individual Jew would succeed in his mission as God's people. Success depended on obedience:

> "'Now then, if you will indeed obey My voice and keep My covenant, then you shall be My own possession among all the peoples, for all the earth is Mine; and you shall be to Me a kingdom of priests and a holy nation.' These are the words that you shall speak to the sons of Israel" (Exod 19:5-6).

Notice the conditional language: *If* they obeyed, *then* they would be a special treasure, a kingdom of priests, and a holy nation.

Sadly, Israel disobeyed. Again and again and again.

God was merciful and patient, but even He had limits. When the covenant was broken, individual Jews—and sometimes whole generations of Jews—could be cut off from the nation (Exod

12:19). The corporate body of Israel was elected, but individuals within Israel could be cut off from the people if they repudiated their election and failed to obey the covenant.

E. Summary

In order to help us understand this evidence, we can organize it along the following lines:

	Who?	Type?	Purpose?
1. Abraham:	Individual	Unconditional	Vocational.
2. Jews:	Corporate	Unconditional	Vocational.
3. Membership:	Individual	Conditional	Vocational.

3. Aaron and the Priesthood

Moses' brother Aaron provides us with another prominent example of someone God chose for an implicitly corporate vocation.

A. God Chose Aaron to Be a Priest

Moses was a reluctant servant. In particular, he complained that he was a bad public speaker who wasn't eloquent or forceful enough to confront Pharaoh. Moses pleaded with God to send someone else. This angered God, but He didn't abandon Moses. Instead, God changed plans and chose Moses' brother Aaron to speak to Israel on Moses' behalf (Exod 4:14-17; cf. Num 17:5). That is a clear example of election to service if ever there was one.

B. Aaron's Election was Vocational

God also chose Aaron to serve as a priest,

> "Did I not *choose* them from all the tribes of Israel *to be My priests*, to go up to My altar, to burn incense, to carry an ephod before Me" (1 Sam 2:28a, emphasis added).

Aaron was given the honor and privilege of serving as the custodian of the altar and the responsibility of teaching Israel its sacred laws (Deut 33:10).

It was a deeply religious and theological calling, but it was not an election to eternal life. Aaron's election was strictly vocational.

C. Aaron's Election Was Corporate

Aaron was chosen as an individual, but his election was also implicitly corporate. In choosing Aaron to be high priest, God was also choosing Aaron's *descendants* to serve as priests after him.

In fact, Aaron's election was *doubly* corporate.

On the one hand, through Aaron, God chose his immediate descendants to be the Aaronites, who were the actual priests. On the other hand, God also chose Aaron's tribe (Levi) to act *as helpers* to the Aaronite priests. The Levites attended to the Aaronites' needs as well as to the needs of the sanctuary but were not allowed to handle the sanctuary vessels or approach the altar (Num 18:2-4, cf., Deut 18:5-8; 21:5; 1 Chron 15:2).

In both cases, the Aaronites and Levites were not chosen for eternal life, but for service.

Their election was vocational.

D. Membership in the Priesthood was Conditional

Earlier, we saw that election is often conditional. The same is true of the priesthood. Not every individual Aaronite or Levite could qualify. Many descendants of Aaron were excluded outright (such as the women, or deformed men, Lev 21:18).

But even those who qualified to serve could have their vocations cut short by an early death if they were disobedient.[1] In fact, that is what happened to Aaron's own sons:

> Now Nadab and Abihu, the sons of Aaron, took their respective firepans, and after putting fire in them, placed incense on it and offered strange fire before the Lord, which He had not commanded them. And fire came out from the presence of the Lord and consumed them, and they died before the Lord (Lev 10:1-2).

---

[1] H. H. Rowley, *The Biblical Doctrine of Election* (London: Lutterworth Press, 1953), 121.

Apparently, this was a recurring problem. Priests would disobey God, fail in their vocation, and God would kill them. The sons of Eli are another example. God killed Hophni and Phinehas because they were disobedient (1 Sam 2:30, 33-34).

The lesson is that when God gives someone a vocation, He holds them accountable to it, and the results of disobedience can be grim.

There can be no mistaking the fact that the priestly vocation was thoroughly vocational and conditional. It was not an election to eternal life. It was an election to service.

E. Summary

God's election of Aaron follows the same pattern we saw with Abraham's election:

	Who?	Type?	Purpose?
1. Aaron:	Individual	Unconditional	Vocational
2. Priesthood:	Corporate	Unconditional	Vocational
3. Membership:	Individual	Conditional	Vocational

4. David and the Kings of Israel

Another famous example of an implicitly corporate individual election was God's choice of David.

Through Abraham, God chose the Jews; through Aaron, the priests; and through David, the kings.

A. *God Chose David to be King*

David wasn't Israel's first king. That responsibility fell to Saul. However, God rejected Saul after he made an unlawful sacrifice (1 Sam 13:8-14) and failed to annihilate the Amalekites as he was commanded (1 Samuel 15). In light of Saul's vocational failure as king, the Lord chose to replace him with David. As David explained to Saul's daughter, Michal,

> "It was before the Lord, *who chose me above your father* and above all his house, *to appoint me ruler* over the people of the Lord, over Israel; therefore I will celebrate before the Lord" (2 Sam 6:21, emphasis added; cf. 1 Kgs 8:16).

Notice that David was chosen for a task, not for eternal life. He was chosen to rule over Israel. His election was vocational.

Notice, too, that David's vocational election happened because of Saul's failure to fulfill his vocation as king. Saul disobeyed God and failed in his duties as king, so God replaced him with David.

B. *Through David, God Chose the Royal Line*

David was chosen as an individual, but God's election was implicitly corporate. When God chose David, it was with a royal line in mind, so He indirectly elected David's house and tribe:

> "Yet, the Lord, the God of Israel, *chose me* from all the house of my father *to be king* over Israel forever. For *He has chosen Judah* to be a leader; and in the house of Judah, my father's house, and among the sons of my father He took pleasure in me to make me king over all Israel (1 Chron 28:4, emphasis added).

C. *Membership in the Royal Line was Conditional*

However, even though David's descendants were chosen to produce the kings of Israel, not every descendant actually became king himself. For example, while David had several sons, only Solomon was chosen to be king:

> "Of all my sons (for the Lord has given me many sons), *He has chosen my son Solomon to sit on the throne* of the kingdom of the Lord over Israel. He said to me, 'Your son Solomon is *the one who shall build My house and My courts*; for I have chosen him to be a son to Me, and I will be a

father to him" (1 Chron 28:5-6, emphasis added).

Please note that Solomon's election was doubly vocational. He was not only chosen to rule over Israel, he was also charged with building the Temple. And as we saw elsewhere, these callings were conditional. Success in his election depended on whether or not Solomon would obey the Lord. Notice the conditional language:

> "I will establish his kingdom forever if he resolutely performs My commandments and My ordinances, as is done now" (1 Chron 28:7).

Sadly, Solomon disobeyed the Lord. He multiplied his wives and worshipped other gods. And the Lord, true to His word, punished Solomon by promising to tear the kingdom away from his son:

> So the Lord said to Solomon, "Because you have done this, and you have not kept My covenant and My statutes, which I have commanded you, I will surely tear the kingdom from you, and will give it to your servant. Nevertheless I will not do it in your days for the sake of your father David, but I will tear it out of the hand of your son" (1 Kgs 11:11-12).

Not even the wisest man who ever lived was exempt from being punished for failing to fulfill his mission.

D. Summary

David's election as king followed the familiar individual/corporate pattern set by God's election of Abraham and Aaron.

	Who?	Type?	Purpose?
1. David:	Individual	Unconditional	Vocational
2. Royal Line:	Corporate	Unconditional	Vocational
3. Membership:	Individual	Conditional	Vocational

5. Conclusion

God's vocational election can be both individual and corporate. When God chose an individual to fulfill a mission—be it as a founding father, priest, or king—He often implicitly chose a group of people to continue the same mission.

So far, we still haven't found a single OT reference to an individual's election to eternal life. God's choices are always to temporal service, not to eternal salvation.

And let me point out something else. Even though Abraham, Aaron, David, and the Jews were uniquely elect, *that doesn't mean God rejected or hated everyone else.*

Let that sink in.

Traditional election is often presented as a great either/or. Either God loves you or He rejects you. Either He chooses you for eternal bliss or for eternal torment.

There is no third option.

Consequently, on that view of election, God's character gets smeared. People correctly wonder—how can a loving and good God possibly create people for the express purpose of torturing them in hell?

In my opinion, a loving God would never do that.

But in any case, a vocational view of election changes the dynamic of that conversation. Instead of calling God's goodness into question, it reveals it.

Vocational election shows that God loves the whole world, including you, and has plans to bless it.

How?

When God elected Aaron, it was not because He hated the other Jews. On the contrary, He wanted to bless all of them by offering a covering for their sins.

When God chose David, it was because Israel needed a godly leader.

When God chose the Jews, it was not because He hated the Gentiles, but to be a blessing to them (Gen 12:1-3).

Simply put, when God chooses people to serve Him, it is usually with the goal of expressing His love for the whole world (John 3:16). Election to service is usually for blessing others. God chooses people, places, and things, for the express purpose of wanting to bless all His creatures, including you.

4

Reward for Service

He who gives great service gets great rewards.
ELBERT HUBBARD

1. Introduction

KEVIN MICHAEL VICKERS WAS the Sergeant-at-Arms of the Canadian House of Commons, responsible for the security of Parliament. It was a position that had been occupied by only ten people since its inception in 1867. For Vickers, it was the culmination of a twenty-eight-year career with the Royal Canadian Mounted Police where he was universally admired as the consummate professional.

On October 22, 2014, those skills would be put to the ultimate test when a Muslim terrorist decided to attack Parliament.

A young Corporal named Nathan Cirillo was
on ceremonial guard duty at the Canadian War
Memorial. He never saw the terrorist who approached from behind and shot Cirillo with a
.30-30 Winchester.

The terrorist then drove to Parliament Hill
where he entered the main buildings and was confronted by security forces. Shots were fired. The
terrorist fled towards the Parliamentary Library
which was next to Vickers's office. Alerted to the
attack, Vickers retrieved a 9mm handgun. When
the terrorist approached, they exchanged fire.
Vickers threw himself to the floor and shot three
times, killing the attacker.

The next day, Vickers went back to work. As
usual, Parliament opened with a procession led by
Vickers. But this time, in honor of the courage he
had shown, Vickers was given an unprecedented
five minute standing ovation from the Members
of Parliament. Throughout the applause and
cheers, Vickers stoically nodded, but said nothing.
He insisted that he had simply done his job. But
the Prime Minister and all of Canada celebrated
him as a hero. In recognition of his professional-
ism and heroism, he was later appointed to be the
Canadian ambassador to Ireland.

We all believe that outstanding service de-
serves to be rewarded. But what about God? Do
you expect Him to reward you for your service?

The topic of divine rewards usually isn't discussed in books on election. That's because most

books on election think of it in terms of heaven or
hell, not in terms of service to God. But once you
see that the OT talks of election in terms of service, you also see there a very strong connection
between service and reward.

We've already seen that God *punishes* those
who fail in their vocations. Now we'll see He also
rewards those who succeed.

2. Rewards Are Natural

The desire to give and receive rewards is
deeply rooted in human nature. There is nothing
more natural than wanting to reward someone
who did a good job for us or went above and
beyond what was required of him. When people
serve us well, we feel a deep sense of gratitude that
naturally spills over into an act of giving (even if
a sense of honor or duty causes us to refuse those
same rewards).

We also see this instinct at work in the OT.

A. Saul and David

Think of the conflict between Saul and David.
When Saul chased David into the wilderness,
intent on killing him, David refused to fight back,
even though he had the opportunity. On several
occasions, David had the chance to kill Saul, but
he didn't. When Saul found out about David's

mercy, his conscience was pricked, and he prayed for the Lord to reward David for sparing his life:

> He said to David, "You are more righteous than I; for you have dealt well with me, while I have dealt wickedly with you. You have declared today that you have done good to me, that the Lord delivered me into your hand and yet you did not kill me. For if a man finds his enemy, will he let him go away safely? *May the Lord therefore reward you with good in return for what you have done to me this day"* (1 Sam 24:17-19, emphasis added).

B. David and Barzillai

Later, when King David and his men were sorely in need of support during the time of Absalom's rebellion, a man named Barzillai rallied to his side. Barzillai was very rich. One writer described him as a venerable, aged, highland chief.

David never forgot the help that Barzillai had given. After Absalom's death, David wanted to reward him for having given him supplies in a time of trouble (see 2 Sam 17:27-29 and 19:31-38).

C. Refusing Rewards

The OT also provides us with examples of prophets who refused rewards for services rendered.

For example, an anonymous man of God was sent to King Jeroboam, denouncing the offerings he made at an altar in Bethel. When the king commanded that the man be arrested, his hand withered. The king begged to be healed and his hand was restored. But when the king invited the man of God to receive a reward, he refused.

> Then the king said to the man of God, "Come home with me and refresh yourself, and I will give you a reward." But the man of God said to the king, "If you were to give me half your house, I would not go in with you; nor would I eat bread nor drink water in this place. For so it was commanded me by the word of the Lord, saying, 'You shall not eat bread, nor drink water, nor return by the same way you came.'" So he went another way and did not return by the way he came to Bethel (1 Kgs 13:7-10).

The man of God was on a mission and it was not part of his divine vocation to be rewarded by the king.

D. Daniel and Belshazzar

Similarly, when Belshazzar made a feast using sacred vessels pillaged from the Temple, a hand appeared and wrote a mysterious message on the wall. Belshazzar was terrified. He summoned

Daniel and promised him great riches and power if he could interpret the writings. Daniel agreed to interpret but adamantly refused the rewards because that was not God's will:

> "Keep your gifts for yourself or give your rewards to someone else; however, I will read the inscription to the king and make the interpretation known to him" (Dan 5:17).

3. General Statements About Divine Rewards

You may not like the concept of rewards. We live in a society in which many think of rewards as a selfish motivation that somehow isn't fitting for true service to God.

God does not share that opinion.

Rewards are Biblical and godly. In His boundless generosity, God loves to reward His servants and give out of His abundance.

The fact that God rewards His servants is found throughout the OT. For example, in Isaiah 40, the prophet says this about God and rewards:

> Behold, the Lord God will come with might,
> With His arm ruling for Him.
> Behold, *His reward is with Him*

And His recompense before Him (Isa
40:10, emphasis added).

This expectation is repeated several chapters
later:

> Behold, the Lord has proclaimed to the
> end of the earth,
> Say to the daughter of Zion, "Lo, your
> salvation comes;
> Behold *His reward is with Him*, and His
> recompense before Him" (Isa 62:11, em-
> phasis added)

God called the people to work for Him and
promised to reward them. The Lord inspired Jeremiah to offer this hope to a restored Israel:

> "Restrain your voice from weeping
> And your eyes from tears;
> *For your work will be rewarded*," declares
> the Lord,
> "And they will return from the land of the
> enemy" (Jer 31:16, emphasis added).

The fact is, keeping God's law was meant to
lead to rewards:

> Moreover, by them Your servant is
> warned; In keeping them *there is great
> reward* (Ps 19:11, emphasis added; cf. Prov
> 13:13).

In sum, God promised to reward the righteous (2 Sam 22:21; Ps 18:20; 58:11). The pattern of reward for service is woven throughout the OT. You cannot miss it.

And more to the point of this book, those rewards are *usually connected to vocational election*. It is precisely those whom God has chosen to do a task who will be rewarded for performing their services well.

4. God Was Abraham's Reward

God chose Abraham to inherit the land of Canaan and to become a great nation. But that promise wasn't fulfilled all at once and it didn't come without effort. Abraham and his descendants were often attacked and had to fight for what was promised.

For example, Abraham's nephew Lot was once captured by an enemy tribe. Abraham rescued Lot from his captors, and in the process recovered some goods and people belonging to Bera, the King of Sodom (Gen 14:14-16).

Bera was evidently both thankful that Abraham had recovered the people, and worried that Abraham would keep the loot for himself, so he offered Abraham a reward. Abraham could keep the goods he recovered in the raid, so long as he returned Bera's people.

But Abraham wasn't interested:

> Abram said to the king of Sodom, "I have
> sworn to the Lord God Most High, pos-
> sessor of heaven and earth, that I will not
> take a thread or a sandal thong or any-
> thing that is yours, for fear you would say,
> 'I have made Abram rich'" (Gen 14:22-23).

God had already promised to make Abraham
rich, and he didn't want Bera to take the credit.
He wanted God to have all the glory. So instead of
keeping the reward, Abraham gave it all back.

That pleased God immensely.

Abraham demonstrated his faith in God's
promise and forsook guaranteed earthly gain
for the hope of God's future blessing. And sure
enough, soon after, the Lord proclaimed that *He
Himself* would be Abraham's "exceedingly great
reward" (Gen 15:1-6).

The key here is to see that the doctrine of
rewards is so central to the OT and so central to
God's own character, that *God Himself is part of
the giving and receiving*! God can give Himself as a
reward for faithful service.

5. The Aaronites' Reward

We know that God chose Aaron and his descendants for the priesthood. In Numbers 18,
we read about their duties, responsibilities, and
rewards. Numbers 18:6 reminds us that the Lev-

ites were chosen by God to perform the service of assisting the priests.

We are also told that the vocation of being a priest was itself a gift from God, a reward for their service:

> "I give your priesthood to you *as a gift for service,* but the outsider who comes near shall be put to death" (Num 18:7b NKJV, emphasis added).

The Levites lived off the tithes given by the other tribes, and that was considered a reward for faithfully fulfilling their vocation in the Temple:

> "You may eat it in any place, you and your households, *for it is your reward for your work in the tabernacle of meeting*" (Num 18:31 NKJV, emphasis added).

6. A Word of Encouragement for King Asa

Here is another example of how vocational election is tied to rewards. Asa was king of Judah for 41 years. We are told he "did what was good and right in the eyes of the Lord" because he removed idolatry from the land and urged his people to seek the Lord (2 Chron 14:2-5). He fulfilled his kingly vocation well.

One day, Asa was attacked by some Ethiopians, but he defeated them against overwhelming odds (2 Chron 14:9-15). The people were jubilant.

So God sent a prophet named Azariah to speak to them.

Azariah assured the people the Lord was with them, so long as they continued to seek Him. But their success was conditional. If they failed to seek Him, the Lord would forsake them again. So Azariah encouraged king Asa to keep up the good work and gave him this advice:

> "But you, be strong and do not let your hands be weak, *for your work shall be rewarded!*" (2 Chron 15:7 NKJV, emphasis added).

God promised King Asa that if he faithfully fulfilled his royal vocation, he would receive a reward. Once again, being chosen to serve is linked to rewards for services rendered.

7. Ruth's Faithfulness

Another example of the OT emphasis on rewards is given to us in the book of Ruth.

After her sons died, Naomi, a Jew, was left with two Gentile daughters-in-law. She encouraged them to move back to Moab. A daughter-in-law named Orpah returned home, but the other daughter-in-law, Ruth, refused to leave. She pledged that Naomi's people would now be her people and that Naomi's God would be her God (Ruth 1:16-17).

When they returned to Bethlehem, they were poverty stricken and needed someone to save them. So Naomi came up with a plan for Ruth to be noticed by Naomi's wealthy relative, a godly man named Boaz. Upon learning of Ruth's devotion to her mother-in-law, Boaz pronounced this blessing upon her:

> And Boaz answered and said to her, "It has been fully reported to me, all that you have done for your mother-in-law since the death of your husband, and how you have left your father and your mother and the land of your birth, and have come to a people whom you did not know before. The Lord repay your work, *and a full reward be given you by the Lord God of Israel,* under whose wings you have come for refuge" (Ruth 2:11-12 NKJV, emphasis added).

He prayed for Ruth to be fully rewarded for fulfilling her vocation as a daughter-in-law.

Ruth wasn't called to be a priest, prophet, or king. She wasn't called to a job that impresses the world. She was simply called to be a faithful daughter-in-law, someone who loved and honored and cared for her mother-in-law. In her service to Naomi, Ruth went beyond what anyone else expected of her. And for that good work, Boaz hoped God would reward her for her service.

The story of Ruth is an example to all of us ordinary believers who seek to fulfill our own vocations in quiet and ordinary ways. God sees your faithfulness. He sees your integrity and your small acts of kindness and He will reward you for it. That's the kind of God He is.

8. Conclusion

In previous chapters, it was hard to miss the Biblical connection between unfaithful service and punishment. I think it is just as hard to miss the connection between faithful service and reward.

When God chooses people to serve Him, He will reward them if they do their job well. That is part of God's divine character and a natural expression of His generosity.

Of course, not every servant does his job well and not all rewards are equal. But no one can doubt that there *are* divine rewards for fulfilling our vocations.

Traditional books about election rarely, if ever, mention this connection. But it will be extremely important to keep in mind once we look at some crucial election passages in the NT.

5

Chosen to Inherit

Say not you know another entirely
till you have divided an inheritance with him.
JOHANN KASPAR LAVATER

1. Introduction

NINA WANG WAS ASIA's richest woman. She
inherited her fortune from her husband Teddy
Wang, who owned Chinachem Group, a major
pharmaceutical company. In 1990, Nina's husband
was kidnapped and never heard from again. She
took over the company and turned it into a major
property developer. When Wang died of cancer
in 2007, her estimated net worth was $4.2 billion.
Since she never had children, the future of her
estate was hotly debated, and two different wills
surfaced.

An earlier will divided up her fortune between family members and a charitable foundation run by Chinachem. But a newer will left Wang's entire fortune to her *feng shui* consultant and secret lover, Peter Chan.

The family cried foul.

Chan was accused of tricking Wang by promising her eternal life in exchange for her fortune. He was arrested and sent to prison for forgery (a charge he denied). However, surprisingly, Chan didn't regret contesting Wang's will or going to prison.

Why not?

As he explained in a letter to his mother, prison led him to Jesus.

As Chan wrote, "God did not promise an eternal blue sky, but He did promise anyone who believes in Him to have eternal life."[1]

Isn't it ironic that a dispute over an earthly inheritance led Chan to faith in Christ for eternal life and an inheritance in the hereafter?

We've looked at OT election and explored its teaching about rewards. There is one more topic I'd like us to examine to help further re-orient our understanding of Biblical election: *inheritance*.

Once again, that may not be the kind of topic you would expect from a book on divine election.

---

[1] Shirley Zhao, "Forger of Nina Wang's Will Peter Chan Compares Self to Apostle in Letter." See http://www.scmp.com/news/hong-kong/article/1402171/forger-nina-wangs-will-peter-chan-compares-self-apostle-letter?page=all. Accessed October 24, 2014.

But maybe you are beginning to see that Biblical election isn't quite the subject that most theologians and philosophers debate about.

2. Hereditary Rights and the First-Born

The Hebrew word for inheritance is *nahela*, from *nahal*, meaning *to inherit or to possess*. It occurs over two hundred twenty times in the OT, most often in the books of Numbers, Deuteronomy, Joshua, Psalms, and Jeremiah.

The Greek translation of the OT (the Septuagint) uses the word *klēros* which originally referred to a lot—a piece of stone or wood—that was drawn and cast with the expectation that the outcome would reflect the will of the gods. Land was divided by lot, such that *klēros* came to refer to that share of the land and eventually took on the meaning of having an inheritance in it.

Of the many occurrences of the word *inheritance*, some have legal and hereditary applications addressing the question of how to divide up family possessions after the death of the head of the house.

A. Property Rights

Many people in the modern world, including many Christians, are suspicious of property. The very idea of accumulating property is thought to be evil. But that isn't the attitude taken in the OT.

The commandment against theft implies we have property rights.

Furthermore, the OT's detailed inheritance laws actually assume that people will have acquired enough property through their lifetime to divide amongst their children after they die (e.g., Num 27:8-11; 36:2-9; Deut 21:15-17).

Not only is it not wrong, in the OT, acquiring property and leaving an inheritance to one's children was a sign of moral uprightness. As Proverbs tells us, "A good man leaves an inheritance to his children's children" (Prov 13:22a).

The idea of having an inheritance is deeply ingrained in the Biblical sense of right and wrong.

For example, when Jacob felt threatened by his father-in-law Laban, he proposed to his wives that they flee with their livestock. Rachel and Leah didn't object to taking the livestock. On the contrary, they considered it their rightful inheritance and the inheritance of their children and urged Jacob to take it all:

> Rachel and Leah said to him, "Do we still have any portion or inheritance in our father's house? Are we not reckoned by him as foreigners? For he has sold us, and has also entirely consumed our purchase price. Surely all the wealth which God has taken away from our father belongs to us and our children; now then, do whatever God has said to you" (Gen 31:14-16).

According to the Law, if a man died without any sons, the inheritance would go to the daughters (Num 27:8-11), so long as they married men from the same tribe (Num 36:2-9).

B. Primogeniture

One of the most theologically noteworthy aspects of OT approaches to inheritance is the principle of primogeniture, i.e., the fact that firstborn sons had greater privileges than other siblings. We can see the theological importance of the firstborn's inheritance at play throughout the Biblical narrative.

For example, patriarchal blessings were often attached to the firstborn son (Gen 25:31; 27:29; 48:13; 49:3). This birthright could either be sold (Gen 25:31, 34) or transferred only so long as it was not because the eldest son was the offspring of an unloved wife (Deut 21:16-17).

There are examples of firstborn sons failing to receive their birthright, such as Ishmael (Gen 17:15–21), Esau (Gen 25:23), and Reuben (Gen 49:3, 4).

It was even possible that, in the absence of a son, a servant could be regarded as an heir, as in the case of Eliezer (Gen 15:2–5).

One of the reasons why primogeniture is theologically important is because Israel is sometimes called God's firstborn:

Then you shall say to Pharaoh, "Thus says the Lord: 'Israel is My son, My firstborn'" (Exod 4:22).

The fact that Israel was God's firstborn means they had the highest possible relationship with God and were the heir to His wealth.

3. God's Inheritance

The concept of inheritance is often employed in an explicitly *theological* sense to describe aspects of the covenantal relationship between God and a people. In fact, God Himself is sometimes described as an inheritor.

A. In People

For example, God is said to have an inheritance in Israel. The Jewish people, having been chosen by God out of all the peoples of the earth, and having been delivered out of Egyptian bondage, belong to the Lord:

> "O Lord God, do not destroy Your people, *even Your inheritance*, whom You have redeemed through Your greatness, whom You have brought out of Egypt with a mighty hand" (Deut 9:26, emphasis added).

In fact, God delivered Israel from the bonds of Egypt so they could belong to Him and not to Pharaoh:

> "But the Lord has taken you and brought you out of the iron furnace, out of Egypt, to be His people, *an inheritance*, as you are this day" (Deut 4:20 NKJV, emphasis added; cf. 9:29 and 1 Kgs 8:51, 53).

B. In the Temple and Holy City

God doesn't only have an inheritance in a people, but the Psalmist also adds that the Temple and holy city are part of God's inheritance (LXX, *klēronomia*):

> O God, the nations have invaded Your inheritance;
> They have defiled Your holy temple;
> They have laid Jerusalem in ruins (Ps 79:1, emphasis added).

C. In the Holy Land

But God does not only own the city and the Temple. Zechariah suggests that God has an inheritance in the entire Holy Land:

> "And the Lord will take possession of Judah *as His inheritance* in the Holy Land, and will again choose Jerusalem" (Zech 2:12 NKJV, emphasis added).

If even God has an inheritance, I hope you'll agree that it is a central category of OT thought.

4. The Jews' Inheritance in the Land of Canaan

Inheritances usually come from our parents, grandparents, or other family members. But people can also receive an inheritance *from God*.

For example, the Lord promised the land of Canaan as an inheritance to Israel:

> "To you I will give the land of Canaan
> as the allotment of your inheritance"
> (1 Chr 16:18, cf. Num 26:53; Josh 18:20;
> Ps 105:11).

As part of Israel's election, God gave them an inheritance in the land. And He promised to drive out the other tribes from the land so the Israelites could live there:

> "Because He loved your fathers, there-
> fore He chose their descendants after
> them. And He personally brought you
> from Egypt by His great power, driving
> out from before you nations greater and
> mightier than you, to bring you in and to
> give you their land for an inheritance, as it
> is today" (Deut 4:37-38).

However, Israel did not receive her inheritance without effort. The book of Joshua records the military victories Israel had to win before settling in the land. Then in Joshua 13 and 14, they divide the land between the tribes, with the Lord noting to Joshua:

> "You are old, advanced in years, and there remains very much land yet to be possessed...Now therefore, divide this land as an inheritance to the nine tribes and half the tribe of Manasseh" (Josh 13:1b, 7 NKJV).

Once in the promised land, each tribe received a portion of land it had to conquer for itself. It was their inheritance, but the land still had to be possessed through obedience, especially through successful military exploits against the native inhabitants.

For example, we read that Caleb inherited Hebron, but he would have to defeat his enemies in order to actually have it:

> "And now, behold, the Lord has kept me alive, as He said, these forty-five years, ever since the Lord spoke this word to Moses while Israel wandered in the wilderness; and now, here I am this day, eighty-five years old. As yet I am as strong this day as on the day that Moses sent me; just as my strength was then, so

now is *my strength for war,* both for going out and for coming in. Now therefore,
give me this mountain of which the Lord
spoke in that day; for you heard in that
day how the Anakim were there, and that
the cities were great and fortified. It may
be that the Lord will be with me, and I
shall be able to drive them out as the Lord
said." And Joshua blessed him, and gave
Hebron to Caleb the son of Jephunneh as
an inheritance. Hebron therefore became
the inheritance of Caleb the son of Jephunneh the Kenizzite to this day, because he
wholly followed the Lord God of Israel
(Josh 14:10-14, emphasis added).

Caleb was old but strong. He was ready for the
challenge that lay ahead. We later read that Caleb
was able to drive out the Gentile families inhabit-
ing the land before him (Josh 15:13-14).

This might surprise you. You might assume
that an inheritance is a *gift* that just comes to you
without any effort at all, but that isn't always the
case even in our own day. After my grandfather
died, it took two and a half years of paperwork,
phone calls, and legal wrangling before the Canadian government released his money (and it
wasn't even very much!). Inheriting took effort.

It took even more effort with the Promised
Land. Out of grace God gave Canaan to the Jews.
But that didn't mean it would be effortless to

attain. The inheritance was promised to God's people, but actually coming into possession of it meant earning it, fighting for it, and risking the possibility of failing to achieve it.

This should come as no surprise. Think of the first generation of Israelites. They left Egypt with the promise of a new land flowing with milk and honey, but soon after entering the wilderness they grumbled against the Lord, disobeyed Him, and were punished with forty years of wandering in the desert. That entire first generation of people (with the exception of Joshua and Caleb) died in exile, without ever entering the land. It was their inheritance, but they failed to attain it.

The lesson here is that an inheritance was not always guaranteed. Possessing it was conditional, just as fulfilling one's vocation was conditional. Success in both depends on obedience and faithfulness to God.

5. Inheriting God

Another important theological meaning of inheritance is the idea that God Himself can be inherited.

A. *The Aaronites*

This is the case with the Aaronites. In Numbers we read,

> Then the Lord said to Aaron, "You shall
> have no inheritance in their land nor own
> any portion among them; *I am your por-
> tion and your inheritance* among the sons
> of Israel" (Num 18:20, emphasis added).

All the other tribes had land and had to fight
to possess it.

But not the Aaronites.

Instead, what they had was a special mission
from God—their vocation.

They had the privilege and gift of being chosen
to serve as priests and of being able to serve God
in His temple on behalf of all the other tribes.

That was their inheritance.

What more could they ask for?

B. The Levites

The Aaronites were the high priests but were
assisted by the Levites. In Deut 14:27, we read that
the tribe of Levi, who were chosen by God for
priestly services for the whole of Israel, would not
have an inheritance in the land of Canaan:

> "Also you shall not neglect the Levite who
> is in your town, for he has no portion or
> inheritance among you" (Deut 14:27).

Instead of land, the Levites' inheritance would
be to live off of the sacrificial offerings brought

by the other tribes. And more importantly, God Himself was said to be their inheritance:

> Therefore, Levi does not have a portion or inheritance with his brothers; *the Lord is his inheritance,* just as the Lord your God spoke to him (Deut 10:9, emphasis added).

C. God as the Inheritance of all Believers

But the Levites were not alone in having God as their inheritance. Though they had the special privilege of serving in proximity to the Lord's own presence on earth, there was a sense in which every Jew could count the Lord as his inheritance:

> The Lord is the portion of my inheritance and my cup;
> You support my lot (Ps 16:5).

> My flesh and my heart fail;
> But God is the strength of my heart and my portion forever (Ps 73:26).

> I cried out to You, O Lord:
> I said, "You are my refuge,
> My portion in the land of the living"
> (Ps 142:5)

These are the prayers that would have been used by believing Jews in their devotions, in the synagogues, and in the Temple service. They expressed the longings, hopes, and faith of the community and so may reasonably be expected to represent the faith of all Jews.

Ultimately, when their inheritance in the land was threatened, or when they were cast into exile, they could still retain the belief that God was their inheritance. Their tie to the Lord was not as directly vocational as the Levites and Aaronites, but He was their inheritance in some sense, because they were the chosen people.

6. Conclusion

The subject of inheritance looms very large in OT thought. And it's an integral part of the Bible's understanding of election.

You cannot fail to notice that *God has an inheritance in the same people, places, and things that He has elected for service.*

In fact, God often elects people, places, and things *precisely so that they might attain an inheritance.*

Inheritance often follows from and is contingent upon one's vocation. This is a pattern we'll see repeated in the NT evidence about election.

6

Human Choices in the Gospels and Acts

You have been chosen, and you must therefore use such strength and heart and wits as you have.
J. R. R. TOLKIEN

1. Introduction

"ASK ME ANYTHING. I know the Torah inside and out."

I was playing a Biblical trivia game with an Orthodox Jewish co-worker. "I've been going to Hebrew school my whole life. Every year we studied a different book from beginning to end. So try me."

I did.

The names of the twelve tribes? Easy. Who killed the guy with the spike through the forehead? Not a problem. How many wives did Moses have? Two, but that's debatable.

She knew her Biblical trivia! Names, dates, places, events. No matter how hard I tried, I couldn't stump her. It made me wish I had gone to Hebrew school.

Do you know who else was immersed in the Torah since childhood? Jesus and the Apostles. They lived and breathed the OT. It informed everything they thought—their language, expressions, habits, culture, and above all, their theology.

That isn't to say they wouldn't have picked up other influences from the Greeks or the Romans. But their beliefs would have been Biblical, absolutely steeped in God's Word. And that includes the Biblical testimony about election.

It would be very surprising if Jesus and the apostles thought about election in a way that was completely different from their forebears. It would be very surprising if the NT doctrine of election departed completely from the deeply vocational OT one in which God chooses people, places, and things to serve His purposes, rewarding the faithful and punishing the unfaithful.

Let's see for ourselves.

2. Meaning

There are several Greek words that are used to indicate God's *choosing* or *electing*. These are *ek-*

legomai, which means *to choose*; *eklektos*, which is the quality of *being elect or chosen*; *eklektoi, the chosen ones*; *epilegō*, to name, call, choose, or select; *haireo,* I choose; *hairetizō*, to choose; and finally, there is the verb *procheirizō*, which means to choose, appoint.

Once again, rather than go over every occurrence of words, we'll look at several significant examples that help clarify and summarize the evidence. As we look at how these words are used in the NT, I think you'll see that it follows very naturally how they are used in the OT.

3. When People Do the Choosing

Let's begin with the human side of election. The Gospels often present people choosing.

A. Choosing the Good Part

For example, when Jesus visited Martha, she was very honored. She did what any good host would do and busied herself making sure that her guests had everything they needed to feel at home.

Mary (Martha's sister) was there, too. But unlike Martha, she didn't help with the housework or the guests. She didn't ask if people were thirsty or hungry. Instead, she just sat and listened to Jesus.

Naturally, Martha got upset. The house was full of people. There were hungry mouths to feed. She needed to set the tables and make sure the dishes were clean. Was there enough bread? Oil? Flour?

Mary! Where's Mary?

Martha expected her sister to pitch in. She didn't. She asked Mary for help. Mary apparently refused. So Martha went to Jesus and asked Him to tell her sister to help serve the guests. Jesus replied:

> "Martha, Martha, you are worried and bothered about so many things; but only one thing is necessary, *for Mary has chosen the good part*, which shall not be taken away from her" (Luke 10:41-42, emphasis added).

What did Mary choose? She chose the *good part*. She chose to listen and to learn.

You'll notice her choice was vocational, i.e. to be a disciple of the Lord.

B. Paul & Silas

Paul and Barnabas had already preached through several cities. People had come to faith and churches were planted. Were they still growing? Paul wanted to find out. "Let us go back and visit the believers in all the towns where we preached the word of the Lord and see how they are doing" (Acts 15:36). Barnabas agreed, but wanted his cousin John Mark to come along (Col 4:10).

Paul didn't like that idea. He had worked with Mark before, and the young man deserted him, so the apostle did not want to take up with him again. But Barnabas insisted. He wanted to give his nephew another chance.

Their disagreement was sharp.

Paul wouldn't go with Mark, and Barnabas wouldn't go without him. They couldn't come to an agreement. Sadly, the two men parted ways. Barnabas and Mark left for Cyprus and disappeared from the Biblical record, whereas Paul continued with his original mission. But he needed help, so he called upon a new companion named Silas:

> But *Paul chose Silas* and left, being committed by the brethren to the grace of the Lord (Acts 15:40, emphasis added).

It should go without saying that Silas was not chosen by Paul to have eternal life. Presumably, he already had it. His election was vocational. Silas was chosen to fulfill a mission for God. John Mark had failed in his vocation. Paul hoped that Silas would not fail in his.

4. Conclusion

The NT depiction of human election mirrors the OT evidence. People either choose vocations for themselves, or are chosen for a vocation.

Either way, when people do the choosing, election is vocational, not for eternal life.

But what about when God chooses? Surely, we'll see an individual election to eternal life now, right?

We'll see in the next chapter.

7

Divine Choices
in the Gospels and Acts

God always gives His best to those who leave the choice with Him.
JIM ELLIOT

1. Introduction

WHEN I WAS A young believer in Montreal, I met a Ukrainian jazz bassist named Yuri. He had terrible scars on both forearms from a suicide attempt. But even though he grew up under Communism, somehow, someway, after his suicide attempt, he became a believer in Jesus Christ. He was proud of those scars because they reminded him of the despair Jesus had saved him from. "This is what happens without Jesus," he said.

At the time he had just arrived in Montreal and was on his way to Toronto to see his sister. He was staying at the YMCA.

Although I tried to help him, the truth was he helped me. I looked at his situation and all I saw was how bad it was. He was homeless, had no money, no job, and no prospects. He had nothing. But to him, he was beyond blessed. He was alive. He was in Canada. Jesus saved him, and the Holy Spirit was with him. He had an incredible sense of gratitude and peace in the purposes of God. He taught me a lesson that I still haven't fully learned twenty years later.

I lost track of Yuri then bumped into him again about a year later. He was playing bass in a touring Gospel band. Little did he know how he affected me spiritually in our short time together.

In the OT we saw that God often chose unlikely people, places, and things to serve His purposes. Election was to service, not eternal life.

Is the NT any different? Does it present God's choosing individuals to go to heaven or hell, paradise or perdition, eternal life or death?

Consider the following examples.

2. God Chose the Jews

In a previous chapter we saw that the single most important OT use of election was in reference to the Jews. They are God's chosen people.

As attested by dozens of OT references, Israel is elect. So it should come as no surprise that we see the same thing taught in Acts:

> "The God of this people Israel *chose our fathers* and made the people great during their stay in the land of Egypt, and with an uplifted arm He led them out from it" (Acts 13:17, emphasis added).

The Jews were chosen by God, and He exalted them. The Greek word for *exalted* (*hupsōsen*) is used elsewhere as the opposite of being humbled (Matt 11:23; Luke 14:11; 18:14) or lowly (Luke 1:52). Luke used it to indicate that Jesus was given the elevated status and honor of being at the right hand of the Father (Acts 2:33; 5:31).

When Luke wrote that God chose the Jewish people and exalted them, he wasn't referring to God's choosing them for eternal life. Rather, he was referring to their prosperity in Egypt where they multiplied and "grew exceedingly mighty; and the land was filled with them" (Exod 1:7). God blessed them economically, socially, and politically.

Eternal life is freely given to all those who believe in Jesus for it (e.g., John 3:16). Every Jew was elect by virtue of being Jewish. The whole Jewish nation was exalted, but not every individual Jew believed in Jesus and became born again (e.g.,

John 12:37). Eternal life and election were two different issues.

3. The Twelve Chosen to Be Apostles

Throughout the OT, from Abraham to Aaron, we saw examples of God's choosing people to serve Him. That same election to service continues in the NT with the choosing of the twelve apostles (who will rule over the twelve tribes, cf. Matt 19:28). In Luke 6:13 we read:

> And when day came, He called His disciples to Him *and chose twelve of them*, whom He also named as apostles (emphasis added; cf. Acts 1:2).

Likewise, in Mark 3:14, we read that:

> *And He appointed twelve*, so that they would be with Him and that He could send them out *to preach* (emphasis added).

What did He choose and appoint the Twelve for? Eternal life? To become regenerate? Is this an example of eternal individual predestination to heaven?

We know this was not an election to eternal life because Judas was among the Twelve and Jesus strongly implied that he was never regenerate: "Did I not choose you, the twelve, and one of you is a devil?" (John 6:70; cf. John 13:10). No devil is regenerate. And yet Judas was just as elect as the other eleven apostles.

Why, then, did Jesus call and appoint the Twelve, if it was not to eternal salvation? Clearly, their election was vocational. They were chosen to serve as apostles[1], specifically to go "out to preach" (Mark 3:14).

The fact that Judas was among those chosen emphasizes our earlier conclusion that election can be *conditional*. You can fail in the mission God has chosen you for, as Judas certainly did. And he knew it.

After Judas committed suicide for his act of betrayal, the apostles needed to find a replacement. But the requirements to be among the Twelve were strict. Potential candidates had to be men who were with Jesus from the beginning. Out of two possible candidates, Matthias was elected by God to become the twelfth apostle (see Acts 1:24: "show which of these two *You have chosen*," emphasis added).

Like the eleven, Matthias was chosen for apostolic service, but nowhere are we told he was elected for eternal life.

---

[1] Roger T. Forster and V. Paul Marston, *God's Strategy in Human History* (Wheaton, IL: Tyndale, 1974), 120.

4. Sent Two by Two

The vocational nature of election is also illustrated by Christ's commissioning of seventy disciples to preach the gospel of the kingdom two by two:

> Now after this *the Lord appointed*[2] seventy others, and sent them in pairs ahead of Him to every city and place where He Himself was going to come (Luke 10:1, emphasis added).

Why were they appointed? Not for eternal life, but for service—to go to every city, preaching, teaching, and preparing the way for Christ.

5. Peter and the Gentiles

You'll remember that by Acts 10, Peter hadn't taken the gospel to the Gentiles. Why would he? Jesus had made it very clear *not* to go the Gentiles (Matt 10:5-6). So after the Ascension, Peter stayed in Jerusalem, preaching, hoping the nation would come to faith in the Messiah. He didn't go to the Gentiles.

Then God sent Peter a vision, telling him to share the gospel with a centurion named Cornelius. Peter resisted at first, then relented. And when he proclaimed the gospel to the centurion,

---

[2] From the verb *anadeiknumi*, I appoint.

Cornelius and his household believed, were filled with the Holy Spirit, and spoke in tongues (see Acts 10). Peter was amazed at what God had done. This is what he later told a conference of elders at Jerusalem:

> Men and brethren, you know that a good while ago *God chose* among us, that by my mouth the Gentiles should hear the word of the gospel and believe. So God, who knows the heart, acknowledged them by giving them the Holy Spirit, just as He did to us (Acts 15:7–8, NKJV, emphasis added).

What was Peter chosen for? Not for eternal life or death. God chose Peter for a particular mission, i.e., that through Peter's preaching the Gentiles would believe the gospel. And the result of the mission was that the Gentiles did believe in Jesus for eternal life. Peter's election *concerned* eternal life (i.e., he was chosen to preach it!), but it was not *to* eternal life. He was chosen to serve.

6. Chosen to be Witnesses

After Jesus rose from the dead, He spent forty days teaching the apostles and disciples about the Messianic kingdom. But He didn't appear to just anyone. He appeared, to witnesses *chosen before[3] by God*, even to us who ate and drank with Him after He arose from the dead (Acts 10:41, emphasis added).

Does that mean these witnesses were individually predestined from timeless eternity to have eternal life?

No.

Jesus appeared to the same apostles, disciples, and preachers who were *previously chosen* to serve Him during His three-year ministry. They needed to know the Messiah rose from the grave and was victorious over death. After Calvary's victory, Jesus was now actually *offering* the kingdom to Israel, not just announcing its imminency.

Hence, these witnesses were *chosen before by God* to see the resurrected Jesus, so they could continue their mission of preaching the good news to Israel (and beyond, cf. Acts 1:8).

7. Saul Chosen to be
the Apostle to the Gentiles

Unfortunately, Israel rejected her Messiah and His offer of the kingdom. Peter offered the kingdom in Acts 3:19, but despite some initial positive responses, by Acts 7 the Jews had so thoroughly rejected Jesus' offer, they stoned Stephen to death.

---

[3] From the verb *procheirotoneo*, I designate beforehand.

What would God do?

Spurned by His chosen people, God started a new work and chose Saul of Tarsus as His new apostle, "born out of due time" (1 Cor 15:8 NKJV).

Many people think that Paul was one of the Twelve.

He was not.

As we read before, God Himself chose Matthias to take Judas' place among the twelve. That's not what Paul was chosen for. Instead, Paul was given a unique office, a unique apostleship. Paul was chosen to be the apostle to the Gentiles:

> But I am speaking to you who are Gentiles. Inasmuch then as I am an apostle of Gentiles, I magnify my ministry (Rom 11:13).

Or, as he vividly describes elsewhere, God chose Paul to use him like a serving dish:

> But the Lord said to him, "Go, for he is a *chosen* instrument of Mine, to bear My name before the Gentiles and kings and the sons of Israel" (Acts 9:15, emphasis added).

Paul was a chosen vessel (*skeuos eklogēs*) to be used for God's own purposes. The word *vessel* also appears in Rom 9:21-23 and emphasizes the vocational nature of Paul's election. He was chosen to accomplish a mission.

Paul's missional election is also emphasized in Acts 22:10; after seeing the vision of the resurrected Jesus, Paul asked, "What shall I *do*, Lord?" Paul knew he was meant to *do* something.

> "And I said, 'What shall I do, Lord?' And the Lord said to me, 'Get up and go on into Damascus, and there you will be told of all that has been appointed[4] for you to do.'"

What was Paul *appointed* to do? To minister among the Gentiles. By the prophetic utterance of one Ananias, Paul was healed and told that he was chosen to preach God's message.

> Then he said, "The God of our fathers *has chosen you* that you should know His will, and see the Just One, and hear the voice of His mouth" (Acts 22:14, emphasis added).

Vocational election is expressed as the reason for Paul and Barnabas's missionary partnership:

> As they ministered to the Lord and fasted, the Holy Spirit said, "Now separate to Me Barnabas and Saul *for the work to which I have called them*" (Acts 13:2, emphasis added).

---

[4] From *tassō*, I appoint.

What were they called to do? Were they called
to have eternal life? No. They were called to work,
i.e., to be missionaries, to evangelize, and to plant
churches.

Finally, Paul's election to service is emphasized
in Acts 26:16. The Lord commanded:

> "But rise and stand on your feet; for I
> have appeared to you for this purpose, *to
> make you a minister and a witness* both
> of the things which you have seen and of
> the things which I will yet reveal to you"
> (emphasis added).

What was the purpose of Jesus' appearing to
Paul? There is no mention of individual predestination to eternal life here. Jesus explains that He
intended to make Paul a minister and witness.
Paul's election was missional.

8. The Sovereignty of God in Election

At this point, let me say a few words about
election and God's sovereignty.

Most in the Calvinist camp define *sovereignty*
as *determinism*. In other words, when they say
God is sovereign, what they mean is that God
causes everything that happens. They think God is
the unilateral cause of all things, including your
every thought and action. As Question 7 of the
Westminster Short Catechism succinctly puts it:

Q: What are the decrees of God?

A: The decrees of God are, his eternal purpose, according to the counsel of his will, whereby, for his own glory, he hath foreordained whatsoever comes to pass.[5]

That definition of sovereignty makes God the author of sin. If God causes everything to come to pass, and sin comes to pass, then God causes sin. There's no avoiding that conclusion.

I don't see that position supported by Scripture, and I don't accept that definition of sovereignty.

Instead, I would say that God is sovereign in the sense of being in *charge* of all things, but not necessarily being in deterministic *control* all things. He is in charge, not in control. What does that mean?

It means God gives people freedom—real freedom. But that freedom is not absolute. It has limits set by God. Moreover, God can override our choices when it suits His purposes. But most of the time our freedom is real, meaning, God does not unilaterally cause what we do or think. For example, God does not cause us to sin, but rightly holds us accountable for the sins we freely choose to commit.

God's sovereignty is also evident in election. So, for example, God is in charge of whom

---

[5] See http://shortercatechism.com/resources/wsc/wsc_007.html. Accessed July 21, 2017.

He chooses to serve. No one tells God whom to choose, and no one has the power to prevent God's choice.[6] In that sense, God is sovereign.

For example, Peter, Andrew, and Matthew did not have the authority to appoint themselves to be Jesus' apostles.[7] That was a sovereign choice that only God could make.

And Peter, Andrew, and Matthew did not have the power to stop God from choosing them to be apostles. That too, was God's sovereign choice.

However, God was not in control of whether or not they would succeed in their vocations. God didn't cause them to behave a certain way but gave them the freedom to be faithful or unfaithful in their service. And sometimes, oftentimes, people choose to fail.

Moses failed. Saul failed. Jonah was unfaithful in his calling as a prophet. Solomon was unfaithful in his calling as a king. And we all know what happened to Judas.

Now, even the freedom to fail has limits. Although many world leaders were free to persecute the Jews, none were free to exterminate them. God has plans that He will accomplish, and He abrogates human choices when it is necessary to accomplish those plans (1 Kgs 22:19-23; Prov 21:1; Dan 4:32; Rev 17:17).

---

[6] Forster and Marston, *God's Strategy*, 120.
[7] Ibid.

Put simply, God is sovereign in the choosing. Man is responsible for the performing. The two complement each other. God is in charge, but He has sovereignly chosen not to be in unilateral control.

9. Conclusion

We have seen that election in the Gospels and Acts is perfectly consistent with the OT evidence.

So far, Biblical election is not the high-minded concept that theologians and philosophers love to debate about, that God selects some individuals for eternal life and others for eternal death. Instead, God's election is practical and mission-oriented. God chooses people for service, to accomplish a task, such as preaching the saving message.

But we're not through looking at the NT yet.

8

Jesus Is the Chosen One

You were the Chosen One!
Obi-Wan Kenobi

1. Introduction

Hollywood loves Messiahs. Whether it's Harry Potter, Frodo Baggins, or Anakin Skywalker, we are enthralled by the story of the Chosen One who must save the world.

Where did that idea come from?

The Bible.

Just go right to the beginning of Genesis, in the Garden of Eden, after the fall of Adam and Eve. That's when God made a promise about a future Messiah. He warned Satan:

> "And I will put enmity between you and the woman, and between your seed and her seed; He shall bruise you on the head,

and you shall bruise him on the heel"
(Gen 3:15).

God promised that Eve would have a Descendant ("her Seed"), Who would bruise the devil's head.

The language is mysterious. Even cryptic. What does "and you shall bruise him on the heel" mean? That isn't immediately clear but it would get clearer over time.

A Messiah was coming, and He Who would save the world from sin and evil.

We know that Messiah was and is Jesus. He is the Chosen One promised in Scripture. Everything was made for Him, through Him, and to Him. Jesus is the center of it all.

The doctrine of divine election is no exception.

If we want to understand what the Bible has to say about election, we need to understand Jesus' elect status.

There are only a handful of verses that explicitly describe Jesus as the Chosen One of God. These are Isa 42:1 (cf. Matt 12:18), Isa 49:7, Luke 23:35, and 1 Pet 2:4, 6.

They are few, but powerful.

Each verse presents us with a different facet of Christ's election, which, when taken together, gives us a better understanding of our own.

2. The Chosen Servant
(Isaiah 42:1; cf. Matthew 12:18)

In Matt 12:18, Jesus is named as the long-awaited Messiah Whose coming was foretold by Isaiah. Indeed, Matthew applies the words of Isa 42:1-4 to Jesus,

> "Behold, My Servant, whom I uphold; *My chosen one* in whom My soul delights" (Isa 42:1, emphasis added).

Jesus is chosen of God. And notice that His election was vocational since He is chosen to be a Servant.

This was not an election to eternal life, but to a mission, i.e., to be the Redeemer of Israel.

3. The Chosen Redeemer

In Isaiah 49-57, we read about the Servant Messiah Who will come to restore God's covenant people to their land. The following verse tells us about the chosenness of the coming Messiah:

> Thus says the Lord, the Redeemer of Israel
> and its Holy One,
> To the despised One,
> To the One abhorred by the nation,
> To the Servant of rulers,
> "Kings will see and arise,
> Princes will also bow down,

Because of the Lord who is faithful, the
Holy One of Israel who *has chosen You*"
(Isa 49:7, emphasis added).

He is chosen. That's clear enough. But Who is
chosen and what is He chosen for?

Earlier in the chapter, Isaiah tells us this Person was chosen to be a Servant (Isa 49:3, 5, 6)
given the task of bringing "Jacob" (a corporate
term for Israel) back to God. As we are told here,
that task would be unsuccessful. "I will have
labored in vain," the Servant exclaims (Isa 49:4).
Nevertheless, He was chosen to labor. His election
is vocational.

In Isa 49:7 the elect person is called *the Redeemer*. By His title alone we know that His election is missional. He is chosen to be the Redeemer
of Israel. But this Redeemer was not given to Israel
alone, but also given to be a light to the Gentiles
(Isa 49:6).

The figure is also said to be "the Servant of
rulers." Although we aren't told *how* he will be the
servant of rulers, it is clearly a vocational calling.

All in all it is abundantly clear the Messiah is
chosen *for service*.

4. The Savior (Luke 23:35)

The fact that Jesus was commonly called or
known as the Chosen One is confirmed by the
taunts of His persecutors,

"He saved others; let Him save Himself if
this is the Christ of God, *His Chosen One*"
(Luke 23:35b, emphasis added).

This verse shows us that even Jesus' enemies
believed in a chosen Messianic figure, even
though they did not believe Jesus was that person.
But they did have Messianic hopes.
They assumed, following Isaiah, that the Messiah had a vocational mission to save people (i.e.,
to redeem Israel). So if Jesus is the Messiah, they
reasoned, He ought to be able to save Himself.
That's the Messiah's mission: saving people.

5. The Living Stone (1 Peter 2:4-6)

Our final verses come from 1 Peter, where
Peter uses an architectural image to show us how
important Jesus is to God's plan for all believers:

> Coming to Him, a living stone—rejected
> by men *but chosen and valuable to God*—
> you yourselves, as living stones, are being built into a spiritual house for a holy
> priesthood to offer spiritual sacrifices acceptable to God through Jesus Christ. For
> it is contained in Scripture:
> "Look! I lay a stone in Zion,
> *a chosen and honored cornerstone,*
> and the one who believes in Him

will never be put to shame!" (1 Pet 2:4-6 HCSB, emphasis added).

My wife and I just recently bought our first house. Going through the process from viewing to closing was quite the learning experience. We came very close to buying an older home, until the inspection report came back with major problems. The owners had built an extension to the house and had done much of the work themselves. To my untrained eye, it looked fine. But the inspection revealed slanted floors, bowed doors, and walls that were slowly separating from the rest of the house. Suffice to say, my wife and I passed!

When you're building a house, you need a plan. That's where the cornerstone comes in. It is the first stone set in constructing a foundation, the one that sets a pattern for all the other stones that you put down afterwards. Every other stone gets placed in reference to that cornerstone. Put down the cornerstone, and you'll know where the front of the house is and where the back is. You'll know whether the house faces east or west, north or south. Put down the cornerstone, and you can orient yourself to the rest of the building.

When Peter calls Christ "a chosen and honored cornerstone," he is saying that God has a plan to build a spiritual Temple, and Jesus is the reference for the rest of us to follow. When Jesus rose from the dead, He became the prototype for what all believers will one day become. And together with Him, we are all being built up like a spiritual temple to God.

When Israel rejected Jesus, it was as though they were rejecting God's entire architectural plan for a new spiritual house. It was as though they were saying God's design was not good enough.

This is not a reference to Jesus' being chosen to have everlasting life. It is a reference to the vocational nature of His election as Messiah. Jesus was sent on a mission to help build a new Temple and a new people for God.

6. Conclusion

Wasn't it ironic that Christ's enemies mocked Him on the cross and took His death as evidence that He was *not* the Messiah? *That was the very mission He was sent to accomplish.*

Jesus was chosen for a mission. He was elected to serve as the Redeemer of Israel and the world.

He was not chosen to have eternal life.

He was not predestined to have eternal life.

On the contrary, Jesus was chosen to be the giver of eternal life to all who believe in Him for it (John 3:16).

Do you believe His promise?

9

The Great Tribulation

*All things are mortal but the Jew;
all other forces pass, but he remains. What is the
secret of his immortality?*
MARK TWAIN

1. Introduction

ONE OF THE GREATEST gifts my parents gave
me was a love of reading. Their bedroom was
dominated by two floor-to-ceiling bookshelves.
One was filled with books on military history (my
dad's). The other was full of Christian books (my
mom's).

As a young boy, I especially loved reading
my dad's books. They were filled with pictures of
guns, tanks, airplanes, and submarines. I dreamt
of serving on a submarine…until I found out
Canada only had four, none of which (at the time)

were even seaworthy or capable of firing torpedoes!

However, those books also had some truly horrific scenes. Photos of the Holocaust, the Gulags, and the Killing Fields, skulls mounted on fences, legs and arms strewn across the rubble of a bombed farmhouse, and bodies heaped by the hundreds in mass graves.

And, of course, there were the Jews. Hair shaved off. Cheekbones protruding beneath sallow eyes. Fabric stars roughly sewn on dirty, torn pajamas.

It was chilling.

Strangely enough, those pictures helped prepare me to believe the truth of Christianity and the Biblical teaching about the End Times. After I became a Christian, I soon learned that, as bad as all the wars in history had been, the worst was still to come. At the end of this age there will be a period of carnage so horrific that all other human catastrophes will pale in comparison.

We call that time the Tribulation.

When Jesus spoke of *the elect,* it was always within the context of His prophecies about the Tribulation (in Matt 24:22, 24, 31; Mark 13:20, 22, 27, and in Luke 18:7). If you want to know who *the elect* are, you need to understand something of those terrible events.

2. The Tribulation in Prophecy

When people think about Jesus, the words *Messiah*, *priest*, and *king* often come to mind. But His status as a *prophet* is not nearly emphasized as much. That is a travesty. Jesus was a great prophet of the end times.[1]

Everyone has heard of Jesus' Sermon on the Mount. Fewer know the Olivet Discourse. It's a little apocalypse, comparable to the Book of Revelation. In it, Jesus gave us important information about how the age will come to an end.

Here is the selection from Matthew 24, in which Jesus mentions the elect:

> "Therefore when you see the 'abomination of desolation,' spoken of by Daniel the prophet, standing in the holy place" (whoever reads, let him understand), "then let those who are in Judea flee to the mountains. Let him who is on the housetop not go down to take anything out of his house. And let him who is in the field not go back to get his clothes…For then there will be great tribulation, such as has not been since the beginning of the world until this time, no, nor ever shall be. And unless those days were shortened, no flesh would be saved; but *for the elect's*

---

[1] See Zane C. Hodges, *The Atonement and Other Writings* (Corinth, TX: Grace Evangelical Society, 2014), 68-109.

sake those days will be shortened. Then if anyone says to you, 'Look, here is the Christ!' or 'There!' do not believe it. For false christs and false prophets will rise and show great signs and wonders to deceive, if possible, *even the elect*...Immediately after the tribulation of those days the sun will be darkened, and the moon will not give its light; the stars will fall from heaven, and the powers of the heavens will be shaken. Then the sign of the Son of Man will appear in heaven... His angels... will gather together His *elect* from the four winds, from one end of heaven to the other" (Matt 24:15–31, emphasis added; cf. Mark 13:20, 22, 27).

Jesus mentions *the elect* three times. Who are they? Although He doesn't explicitly tell us, He does give us a clue. Jesus began by referring to *a sign* "spoken of by the prophet Daniel" and the Gospel writer quickly added, "whoever *reads*, let him understand." Clearly, Jesus was telling His hearers that if they wanted to understand what He was saying (and who the elect are), they needed to read Daniel. Indeed, comparing the two make the identity of the elect very clear.

3. Daniel's Sign

First of all, what "sign" was Jesus referring to in Daniel?

Daniel called it the "abomination of desolation" and spoke of it three times (Dan 9:27; 11:31; 12:11). Many scholars think the "abomination of desolation" was fulfilled by Antiochus Epiphanes (215 BC–164 BC),[2] a Greek king who attacked Jerusalem, outlawed Judaism, and tried to impose idolatry on the land. His ultimate act of sacrilege, the one considered "the abomination of desolation," occurred when he erected a statue of Zeus in the Temple and sacrificed a pig on its altar.[3] That kind of desecration of the Temple was probably the sign Jesus implied would happen again in the future.

It is hard for us to imagine the horror of that act.

For the Jew, the Temple was the center of the entire universe, the place where God Himself lived, and where humanity came to be forgiven by God. So when Antiochus desecrated the Temple, he was doing more than just shaking the proverbial fist at Israel's God. He was jeopardizing humanity's connection with God and showing his disdain of the Lord's religious, moral, and political order.

---

[2] The incident was recorded in 1 Maccabees 1:44-54.
[3] James A. Brooks, *Mark* (Nashville, TN: Broadman Press, 1991), 212.

Imagine if terrorists blew up the Statue of Liberty, the Smithsonian, the White House, and Cowboys Stadium, and then multiply that by a thousand times, and maybe you'll understand how outrageous Antiochus's actions were.

Suffice to say, Antiochus's actions served as a type for all future desecrations of the Temple.[4]

4. The End Comes to Israel

The fact that Jesus spoke of a still future abomination of desolation shows that He did not think Antiochus completely fulfilled Daniel's prophecies.

In particular, some of the events of the Third Prophecy (Dan 9:24-27) have yet to come to pass. Hence, in the Olivet Discourse Jesus told people to look for a desolating sacrilege *still to come.*

Here is the passage in Daniel that Jesus was referring to:

> "He will make a firm covenant
> with many for one week,
> but in the middle of the week
> he will put a stop to sacrifice and offering.
> And *the abomination of desolation*
> will be on a wing of the temple

---

[4] Ibid., 212. See also, *The Popular Bible Prophecy Commentary*, eds. Tim Lahaye, Ed Hindsen (Eugene, OR: Harvest House, 2006), 258-259.

until the decreed destruction
is poured out on the desolator" (Dan 9:27
HCSB, emphasis added).

The setting is Israel, in particular, the Temple in Jerusalem. The "he" that Daniel spoke of is a future world ruler (see Dan 9:26). This world ruler "will make a firm covenant" with Israel, presumably establishing peace in the Middle East lasting for one prophetic "week" (or heptad), in which each prophetic "day" unit represents a year, for a total of seven years.

However, Daniel warns that "in the middle of the week"—that is, after three-and-a-half years of unprecedented peace in the Middle East—this world ruler will reveal his true character by putting "a stop to sacrifice and offering" in the Temple. And then, like Antiochus Epiphanes, the Antichrist will erect "the abomination of desolation" and desecrate the Temple. As John Walvoord explains,

> "Just as Antiochus Epiphanes in the second century B.C. desecrated the temple in Jerusalem by offering a sow on the altar and setting up an idol of a Greek god, so in the end time the final world ruler, who will claim to be God, will set up an image of himself and constitute the abomination of the temple."[5]

---

[5] John F. Walvoord, *Every Prophecy of the Bible* (Colorado Springs, CO:

In sum, Jesus warned His listeners that a future ruler would desecrate the Temple, most likely by sacrificing a sow upon the altar, after which people can expect the "great tribulation, such as has not been since the beginning of the world until this time, no, nor ever shall be" to begin. Daniel also described the event in chapter 12:

> "Now at that time Michael, the great prince who stands guard over the sons of your people, will arise. *And there will be a time of distress such as never occurred since there was a nation until that time*; and at that time your people, everyone who is found written in the book, will be rescued. Many of those who sleep in the dust of the ground will awake, these to everlasting life, but the others to disgrace and everlasting contempt. Those who have insight will shine brightly like the brightness of the expanse of heaven, and those who lead the many to righteousness, like the stars forever and ever" (Dan 12:1-3, emphasis added).

Daniel spoke about a time of trouble "such as never occurred since there was a nation until that time." Jesus obviously evoked the same event. Jews called this period the time of "Jacob's Trouble." Christians call it the Tribulation.

Chariot Victor Publishing, 1999), 257.

5. Daniel's People

One difference between Daniel's prophecy and Jesus' Olivet Discourse is the terminology. While Jesus spoke about "the elect," Daniel spoke about the "sons of your people" and "your people." Were Jesus and Daniel talking about the same group?

Yes, they were.

Daniel used the phrase *your people* no less than eight times, and it is absolutely clear that he was referring to the Jews. For example:

"And now, O Lord our God, who have brought *Your people* out of the land of Egypt with a mighty hand" (Dan 9:15a, emphasis added). Whom did God bring out of Egypt? The Jews.

Daniel also explained that: "*Jerusalem and Your people* have become a reproach to all those around us" (Dan 9:16b, emphasis added).Which people are most closely associated with Jerusalem? The Jews.

And lastly, Daniel refers to "Your city and *Your people* are called by Your name" (Dan 9:19b, emphasis added). Which city and people are called by God's name? Obviously, it is Jerusalem and the Jews.

In short, there should be no doubt that when Daniel says that *your people* shall be delivered from the unprecedented time of trouble—i.e., will be saved from an early death during the Tribulation carnage—he is talking about *the Jewish people*.

6. Jesus and the Elect

Jesus was not teaching about individual election to eternal life. When Jesus said that "those days will be shortened" for the "elect's sake," He was undoubtedly teaching the Tribulation would be shortened for the sake of preserving the Jews from complete annihilation. As Hal Haller confirms: "The terminology refers to *the preservation of Israel* (i.e., the elect) to the end of the Tribulation…God will shorten that time of genocidal persecution so that *Israel's* persecutors will be unable to destroy her." [6]

However, Daniel didn't say that every single Jew would be preserved from dying during the Tribulation, but only those "found written *in the book*" (Dan 12:1, emphasis added). Daniel was referring to *the Book of Life* (e.g., Rev 20:11-15) which records the names of everyone who has received everlasting life through faith in Jesus. We know that Daniel has everlasting life in view, because the next verse involves a future bodily resurrection, "Some to everlasting life, some to shame and everlasting contempt" (v 2b).

In other words, Daniel and Jesus were teaching that God would shorten the Tribulation in order

---

[6] Hal M. Haller, "Matthew," *The Grace New Testament Commentary* (Denton, TX: Grace Evangelical Society, 2010), 1:112.

to preserve the Jewish remnant who will come to faith during the Tribulation.

7. The Avenged (Luke 18:7)

Now that we have a better grasp of Jesus' words in Matthew 24 (cf. Mark 13), we are in a much better position to understand what the Lord said in Luke 18:7:

> "now, will not God bring about justice for *His elect* who cry to Him day and night, and will He delay long over them?"

Whom does the Lord mean in speaking of *the elect*? Once again, it refers to the Jewish remnant during the Tribulation period, those who have believed in Christ for eternal life.[7] God will avenge His elect people. This isn't a statement about individual predestination to eternal life. It is just a reiteration that God has a chosen people, and He will do right by them.

8. Conclusion

When Jesus prophesied about *the elect* during the Olivet discourse, He wasn't referring to individuals whom God has chosen from all eternity to

---

[7] William MacDonald, *Believer's Bible Commentary*, ed. Art Farstad (Dallas, TX: Thomas Nelson, 1989), 1438.

have eternal life. Rather, He was using the familiar term for God's people, the Jews.

In particular, Jesus was prophesying about a remnant within Israel, Jews who will come to faith during the Tribulation. They will be gathered, preserved, and kept by God through that horrific time.

To answer Mark Twain's question, the secret to the Jew's immortality is God's providence.

10

Many Are Called, But Few Are Chosen (Matthew 22:14)

*"Know first who you are,
and then adorn yourself accordingly."*
EPICTETUS

1. Introduction

WHEN PRINCE WILLIAM MARRIED Kate Middleton, millions of well-wishers watched the ceremony on TV, but only nineteen hundred people attended it in person at Westminster Abbey. You can imagine what an honor it was to be invited. The Queen's lunchtime reception at Buckingham Palace was even more exclusive with only six hundred fifty people invited. And smaller still was the dinner at Buckingham Palace, given by the

Prince of Wales, where only three hundred people attended.[1]

In other words, the royal wedding wasn't a single event, but actually consisted of several events, with different levels of privilege, honor, and exclusivity tied to each. Getting invited to one did not mean you were automatically invited to all three.

Did you know that when Jesus described life after death, He compared it to a royal wedding feast?

In fact, the Bible often used banquet imagery to depict the Messianic kingdom (see Ps 22:26-29; Isa 25:6-9; 65:8-16; Rev 19:6-9).[2] And that's how Jesus depicted it in the Parable of the Wedding Feast, which He concluded with this cryptic comment:

> "For many are called, but few are chosen" (Matt 22:14).

What did Jesus mean? How are they called? Who are chosen? And why so few?

Although that verse has often been taken to teach individual election to eternal life, that interpretation does not fit the context.

---

[1] http://www.telegraph.co.uk/news/uknews/royal-wedding/8469683/Royal-wedding-guest-list-who-will-be-attending-Prince-William-and-Kate-Middletons-big-day.html. Accessed December 23, 2015.
[2] Gregory P. Sapaugh, "A Call to the Wedding Celebration: An Exposition of Matthew 22:1-14," in *JOTGES* 51 (Spring 1992): 11-34.

2. Kingdom Rewards

As I said, the key phrase occurs at the end of the parable. Here is the second half:

> "But when the king came in to look over the dinner guests, he saw a man there who was not dressed in wedding clothes, and he said to him, 'Friend, how did you come in here without wedding clothes?' And the man was speechless. Then the king said to the servants, 'Bind him hand and foot, and throw him into the outer darkness; in that place there will be weeping and gnashing of teeth.' *For many are called, but few are chosen*" (Matt 22:11-14, emphasis added).

I think one of the reasons why this passage is often misunderstood is because few theologians recognize there will be a literal Messianic kingdom with different levels of privilege and reward within it.

And yet, that is what Jesus taught.

For example, Jesus said that Israel would receive a literal kingdom. Not a metaphorical one. Not one that was already realized during His ministry. But a literal, future, kingdom.

Jesus preached that message throughout His ministry and after the resurrection, spent another forty days teaching the disciples about the kingdom (Acts 1:3). In fact, their last question to Jesus tells us what He promised them:

> "Lord, is it at this time You are restoring the kingdom to Israel?" (Acts 1:6b).

Clearly, Jesus taught, and the apostles expected, a literal kingdom for Israel that had not yet arrived, but which, based on what Jesus just taught them, would be restored sometime in the future.

Jesus also taught that eternal rewards based on their good works would be given in the kingdom.

> "And behold, I am coming quickly, and My reward is with Me, to give to every one *according to his work*" (Rev 22:12, emphasis added).

Crucially, Jesus also spoke of a specific privilege of *ruling with Him in the kingdom*. For example, Jesus assured the apostles:

> "Assuredly I say to you, that in the regeneration, when the Son of Man sits on the throne of His glory, you who have followed Me will also sit on twelve thrones, judging the twelve tribes of Israel" (Matt 19:28).

The Messiah wasn't going to rule alone but would have companions (Ps 45:7; Luke 19:11-27; Heb 1:9).

In the Parable of the Minas we learn that Jesus is coming back with His kingdom and He'll be looking for *servants to rule with him*:

> "And he said to him, 'Well done, good slave, because you have been faithful in a very little thing, you are to be in authority over ten cities'" (Luke 19:17; cf. vv 11-27).

God's goal has always been for man to rule over creation (Gen 1:26), and after the fall, the OT provides many examples of godly servants who are elevated to positions of rulership over a kingdom (e.g., Joseph, Moses, David, Esther, Daniel, etc.). The apostles understood that. That was their goal, too, which is why James and John asked Jesus,

> "Grant that we may sit, one on Your right and one on Your left, in Your glory" (Mark 10:37).

The apostles wanted to rule with Christ at His right hand.

Likewise, Paul assured Timothy that:

> If we endure, *we shall also reign with Him*" (2 Tim 2:12a, emphasis added).

Reigning with Christ in the kingdom is the reward for enduring in the faith. But it's also conditional, as Paul went on to warn,

If we deny Him, He also will deny us
(2 Tim 2:12b).

What will Jesus deny unfaithful believers? This is not about eternal salvation, but about the privilege Paul has just said would be granted to overcomers, i.e., *to reign with Him*. If you do not endure, you will be denied reigning with Christ. That is exactly what Jesus taught in the Parable of the Minas.

> "Then he said to the bystanders, 'Take the mina away from him and give it to the one who has the ten minas.' And they said to him, 'Master, he has ten minas already.' I tell you that to everyone who has, more shall be given, but from the one who does not have, even what he does have shall be taken away" (Luke 19:24-26).

Knowing that eternal rewards and privileges can be won or lost depending on our good deeds puts the wedding guest in new light.

3. Getting Thrown Out of the Party

The Bible uses vivid and varied imagery to depict the possibility of losing eternal rewards.

For example, Jesus talked about having our investments and cities taken away (Luke 19:12-27).

Paul sometimes talked about having our work burned up just as a farmer burns hay, straw, and stubble (1 Cor 3:11-15), or being disqualified from a sporting event (1 Cor 9:26-27). Let me suggest that being thrown out of an exclusive wedding banquet is another picture of losing eternal rewards.

Consider how the guest is described:

> "But when the king came in to look over the dinner guests, he saw a man there *who was not dressed in wedding clothes*, and he said to him, 'Friend, how did you come in here *without wedding clothes*?' And the man was speechless. Then the king said to the servants, 'Bind him hand and foot, and throw him into the outer darkness; in that place there will be weeping and gnashing of teeth.' For many are called, but few are chosen" (Matt 22:11-14, emphasis added).

The man was not wearing the proper wedding clothes, which angered the king.

Why?

Why is lacking the proper clothes bad? What do the clothes represent?

To answer those questions, consider the following passage from Revelation which also describes the garments worn to the Messianic banquet:

> "Let us be glad and rejoice and give Him glory, *for the marriage of the Lamb has come*, and His wife has made herself ready." And to her it was granted to be arrayed in *fine linen*, clean and bright, *for the fine linen is the righteous acts of the saints* (Rev 19:7-8, emphasis added; cf. Ezek 44:17).

What do the clothes represent? In this passage, to be dressed in fine linen means being clothed in righteous acts.

I think that's what the wedding garments symbolized in Jesus' parable. That's why the king was upset. It was the guest's responsibility to come properly dressed—i.e., to have lived a life worthy of reward—and he failed. So he was denied the privilege of eating at the royal banquet.

In support of the interpretation that this concerns eternal rewards, not eternal life, consider that the guest *is in the kingdom*. Why is that significant? Because Jesus said only people who are born again will see the kingdom:

> "Truly, truly, I say to you, unless one is born again he cannot see the kingdom of God" (John 3:3b).

So the guest was born again. He was in the Messianic kingdom. His problem was not lack of eternal life, but lack of eternal reward. He was not qualified to attend the banquet, so he was tossed out of the party into the outer darkness.

Where is the outer darkness? This is not hell, but "the darkness outside the limits of the lighted palace."[3] It may help to remember that Jewish wedding banquets would happen at night (as many wedding receptions also do today). So this is the darkness *outside the brightly lit wedding hall,* not hell, hades, or the lake of fire.

And what does the "weeping and gnashing of teeth" mean? That's *not* a special expression for the pains of hell, but a general Semitic expression of grief and shame appropriate for many occasions. In this case, it is the shame of being publicly embarrassed, found unworthy to stay at the celebration, and kicked out of the wedding hall.

Did you know it is possible for believers to feel shame at Christ's coming? Shame for the way you might have wasted your life, instead of serving Him? That's what John warned his born-again "little children" about:

> Now, little children, abide in Him, so that when He appears, we may have confidence and not shrink away from Him in shame at His coming (1 John 2:28).

---

[3] However, Thayer goes beyond the lexical evidence to offer the theological opinion that the palace represents the entire Messianic kingdom. Joseph H. Thayer, *Thayer's Greek-English Lexicon of the New Testament* (Peabody, MA: Hendrickson Publishers, 1896, 2000), 226.

If you've been faithful to Christ in this life, you'll feel no shame at His coming.

If you haven't been faithful—if you've been a poor steward of the time and gifts He's given you. If you've wasted your time on wanton pursuits, laying up treasure on earth, rather than in heaven, then there is a real possibility that you'll feel shame at having all your works of wood, hay, and straw burned up.

4. The Called and the Chosen

When Jesus ended the parable by saying that "many are called, but few are chosen," He was criticizing and challenging the Jewish religious leaders' vocation and authority. Like the apostles, the Jewish Establishment assumed they would be ruling with Messiah in His kingdom. Instead, Jesus warned that tax collectors, harlots, and other people gathered in the "highways" would replace them.

The "calling" refers to Israel's calling to rule with Messiah as His companions. This is what Israel was elected to do, especially the religious leaders. But as we saw in previous chapters, success in her calling was conditional, not guaranteed. There was a possibility of failure, as the OT illustrates time and time again. Sadly, religious leaders who confronted Jesus were repeating that history of failure.

While all of Israel is called to rule with the Messiah, only a few will be "chosen" to enjoy those privileges. As Zane Hodges explains:

> The Savior's parable is a magnificent metaphor. It visualizes the kingly joys of God's Son under the familiar Old Testament image of wedding celebration. The invited guests are called to participate in these joys, and their wedding garments are symbols of their successful efforts to prepare themselves for these.
>
> But the man who lacked the garment was unprepared for such special privileges…Like the servant who hid the mina (Luke 19:26), the man is not allowed to be active for his Lord in the experience of joint heirship. The darkness outside is a powerful, evocative image for the exclusion he experiences as a result.[4]

5. Conclusion

Matthew 22:14 is not about how God elects individuals for eternal life or death, but how personally righteous believers will be rewarded in Jesus' kingdom.

---

[4] Zane C. Hodges, *Grace in Eclipse: A Study on Eternal Rewards* (Corinth, TX: Grace Evangelical Society, 2016), 127.

In particular, the context strongly suggests Jesus was warning the Temple priests and religious leaders that they were failing in their vocations and would not be qualified to attend the Messianic banquet. Attending that banquet would be reserved for believers who have clothed themselves with acts of righteousness. As Joseph Dillow summarizes:

> According to the Lord, many are called to personal salvation and to enter the banquet, but only the faithful will be admitted to the wedding feast of the Lamb…
> the context is about being chosen (based upon righteous deeds) to participate in a celebration, and the issues of election and predestination are not in view at all.[5]

As amazing and as honoring as it must have been to attend Prince William and Princess Kate's wedding, the rewards of Jesus' kingdom, including attending His wedding banquet, will be far greater.

---

[5] Joseph C. Dillow, *Final Destiny: The Future Reign of the Servant Kings* (N.P.: Grace Theology Press, 2013), 796.

11

You Have Not Chosen Me
(John's Gospel)

*Always render more and better service than is
expected of you, no matter what your task may be.*
OG MANDINO

1. Introduction

DO YOU REMEMBER WHEN it was time to give
oral presentations in class?

It was always nerve-wracking for me.

When the teacher picked up her list of names
and started randomly choosing who would go
next, I would begin doing my best to avoid being
noticed, but never knew how best to be incon-
spicuous. Should I stare at the ceiling or look at
the ground? Should I look busy going through my
notes or look her in the eyes very calmly?

Any which way, it was nerve-wracking.

I wonder how the disciples felt to have been chosen by Jesus.

Were they nervous?

Were they excited?

Was it amazing, humbling, or awesome to have the Son of God come to you, look you in the eyes, point his finger, and say, "Follow Me"?

John's Gospel records four examples of Jesus' speaking about choosing people (John 6:70; 13:18; 15:16, 19). Not a single one refers to being individually elected for eternal life or death. Each is an example of Jesus' choosing someone, usually an apostle, for service.

2. Did I Not Choose You?

In John 6, Jesus declared that He had chosen the twelve apostles:

> Jesus answered them, "Did I not choose you, the twelve, and one of you is a devil?" (John 6:70).

This was clearly not an individual election to eternal life, because one of the Twelve—Judas— was a devil, and that's hardly the kind of language used to describe the regenerate (cf. John 13:10-11, 18). And yet Jesus is affirming that Judas was just as chosen as the others.

Moreover, the Lord chose Judas, knowing that He would betray Him. In his own way, Judas was chosen to serve, too. In this case, to fulfill Scripture. He would betray the Lord just as Ahithophel had once betrayed David and later hanged himself (cf. 2 Sam 16:20–17:3, 23; Ps 41:9).

3. Chosen to Bear Fruit

In John 15, the point is made again that the apostles were chosen by Jesus for a mission.

> "You did not choose Me, but I *chose you* and appointed you *that you should go and bear fruit*, and that your fruit should remain, that whatever you ask the Father in My name He may give you" (John 15:16, emphasis added).

Notice that Jesus compares and contrasts His choice of the apostles with their choice of Him. That's significant because it suggests those choices happened on the same level, that they're the same kind of election. As Lenski explains,

> The negation, "you did not choose me," is proof that the affirmation, "I did choose you," cannot refer to predestination but must refer to the choice of the disciples as the friends whom Jesus selected for himself (middle voice) for the apostleship.[1]

---

[1] R. C. H. Lenski, *The Interpretation of St. John's Gospel* (St Louis, MO: Augsburg, 1963), 1051.

The apostles, Judas included, obviously did
not choose Jesus for eternal life because the Lord
doesn't need it—He *is* life, the very source of eternal life (John 1:4; 11:25; 14:6). Rather, the apostles
accepted the invitation to follow Jesus on His
Messianic mission.

So what did Jesus choose the apostles for? Not
for eternal life, but to complete a mission in His
service.[2] As Jesus says, they were chosen to "bear
fruit" for Him in preaching the gospel of the kingdom.

4. Chosen Out of the World

> "If you were of the world, the world would
> love its own. Yet because you are not of
> the world, but *I chose you* out of the world,
> therefore the world hates you" (John
> 15:19, emphasis added).

When were the apostles chosen "out of the
world"? It wasn't during a moment before time
and space in the predestining mind of God.
Rather, it was a this-worldy election, in time, not
in eternity past. As Lenski argues, "The context
forbids that we think of an act taking place in
eternity; this choice occurred when the disciples

---

[2] Edwin A. Blum, "John," *The Bible Knowledge Commentary: New Testament*, eds. John F. Walvoord and Roy B. Zuck (Colorado Springs, CO:
Chariot Victor, 1983), 326.

were drawn to Jesus."[3] When they were drawn to the Lord, they left their mundane vocations behind in order to pursue an evangelical mission.[4] As Moulton and Milligan comment, this choice had

> "nothing to do with eternal predestination, but only with choosing them out of the world after they were in it. He had 'appointed' them, and put them into the position which they were to occupy on their post of duty...This can be nothing else but their going out into the world to take His place, to produce fruit to the glory of the Father, and to return with that fruit to their Father's house."[5]

They were apostles chosen to serve, to bear spiritual fruit,[6] and to share the gospel promise as ambassadors for Christ (cf. 2 Cor 5:20). And Jesus warned them that the world would hate them for it. They would represent Christ, and would be rejected for it, because so much of the world hates the light, and loves darkness. So the apostles had to be prepared to suffer for His service.

---

[3] Lenski, *John*, 1055-56.
[4] John F. Hart, "John," *The Moody Bible Commentary*, eds. by Michael Rydelnik and Michael Vanlaningham (Chicago, IL: Moody, 2014), 1651.
[5] Quoted in Samuel Fisk, *Election and Predestination: Keys to a Clearer Understanding* (Bicester: Penfold Book and Bible House, 1997), 105.
[6] John F. Parkinson, *The Faith of God's Elect: A Comparison Between the Election of Scripture and the Election of Theology* (Glasgow: Gospel Tract Publishers, 2007), 77.

5. Jesus Draws All

In addition to the verses above, John 6 contains some sayings of Jesus that have been interpreted to teach individual election to eternal life.

If you'll recall, a large crowd had followed Jesus, and He miraculously fed them with a little boy's humble lunch. After that sign, they continued to follow Him, though, perhaps, not for the right reason:

> Jesus answered them and said, "Truly, truly, I say to you, you seek Me, not because you saw signs, but because you ate of the loaves and were filled (John 6:26).

Given the thousands of people who were seeking Him, Jesus said:

> "No one can come to Me unless the Father who sent Me draws him; and I will raise him up on the last day" (John 6:44).

The problem with taking this verse as teaching that God only elects *some* individuals to eternal life, is that John's Gospel makes very clear that God is drawing *all men* to Jesus.

Jesus is the "Light of men" who "enlightens every man" so that "all through him might believe" because God loves "the world" (John 1:4, 9, 7; 3:16). Jesus is very clear that all men are being drawn:

"And I, if I am lifted up from the earth,
will draw *all men* to Myself" (John 12:32,
emphasis added).

So while it is true that "no one can come" to
Jesus without the Father's drawing, it is also true
that "all men" are drawn. No exceptions. In other
words, Jesus is teaching that God is the One Who
always takes the initiative in salvation. You might
have thought that God was silently waiting for you
to find Him of your own accord, but the truth is
God was drawing you long before it ever occurred
to you to start looking.

However, that drawing is *resistible*. Just because everyone is drawn does not guarantee that
everyone will actually *believe* in Jesus for everlasting life. Jesus tells us in no uncertain terms that
some people do not believe, not because God has
not drawn them, but because they were unwilling
to come.

"and you are unwilling to come to Me so
that you may have life" (John 5:40).

As George Bryson argues,

Here our Lord specifically tells us why
these men did not have the Father's Word
abiding in them. It was not because they
were not elect or that they were not ir-
resistibly or effectually called. It was not
because they had not been subjected to

irresistible grace. It was because they inexcusably did not believe in God's Son. Here our Lord tells us why they could not have eternal life. It was not for any of the reasons Calvinism suggests. Rather it was because they were not willing to come to God's Son in faith.[7]

In sum, John 6:44 does not teach individual election to eternal life. Rather, Jesus is teaching that before you came to faith in Jesus, God was already drawing you, and all men, to His Son. But that drawing is resistible. Those who do not finally come to faith in Jesus have no one to blame but themselves.

6. All That the Father Gives

If Christ's drawing is resistible, why, then, does Jesus also say in John 6, "All *that* the Father gives Me *will* come to Me"? In that case, the giving seems irresistible and unconditional. And it is. But this is not about individual election to eternal life. To see why, consider the whole passage.

"All *that* the Father gives Me will come to Me, and the one *who* comes to Me I will certainly not cast out. For I have come down from heaven, not to do My own

---

[7] George Bryson, *The Dark Side of Calvinism* (Santa Ana, CA: Calvary Chapel Publishing, 2004), 202-203.

will, but the will of Him who sent Me.
This is the will of Him who sent Me, that
of all that He has given Me I lose nothing,
but raise it up on the last day. For this is
the will of My Father, that *everyone who*
beholds the Son and believes in Him will
have eternal life, and I Myself will raise
him up on the last day" (John 6:37-40,
emphasis added).

Notice that I emphasized the pronouns.
In his article, "Is John 6:37-40 'Frankly
Predestinarian?'"[8] Randy White points out there is
a grammatical difference between the neuter pronoun *that* (*ho*) and the masculine pronoun *who*.
John correctly and consistently uses *that* to refer
to *things*, and *who* and *whom* to refer to *people*.
Hence, White believes the switch in gender, from
neuter to masculine, is deliberate, and essential to
properly understanding the passage.

So what do the respective pronouns refer to?
White argues *that* refers to the nation of Israel,
while whereas *who* refers to individual believers.

Remember the individual/corporate pattern
in election we explored in chapter 3? We saw that
God can unconditionally elect a corporate body,
but any particular individual's participation in
that body can be conditional. That same dynamic
is at play in this passage. As White says,

---

[8] See https://randywhiteministries.org/articles/john-637-40-frankly-
predestinarian. Accessed July 28, 2017.

Jesus is teaching something both about
the national inheritance He has in Israel
and something about the individual in
the crowd who would not reject Him but
come in faith then and there.[9]

White points out that, according to the Bible,
the inheritance that God gives to Messiah is the
nation of Israel (Deut 7:6, 14:2, 26:19; Exod 19:5-
6; Ps 50:5; Jer 2:3; Amos 3:2; Mal 3:17). The neuter
that refers to Israel as a corporate body, which
Jesus will unconditionally receive as His inheritance.

However, individual participation in Israel
depends upon a person's faith. The masculine *who*
refers to those believers.

When Jesus said, "All *that* the Father gives Me
will come to Me," He was speaking about Israel
and saying that He will receive Israel as His unconditional inheritance as Messiah.

When Jesus went on to say, "and the one *who*
comes to Me I will certainly not cast out," He
was speaking about individual people coming to
believe in Him. If they did, they would be born
again, and eternally secure, from the moment of
faith. As White summarizes:

even though the nation (God's inheritance) was rejecting Jesus, that nation
would not be lost. Rather, Christ would

---

[9] Ibid.

"raise it up on the last day." As Paul says, in the end "all Israel will be saved" (Romans 11:26). But what of the individual in Christ's day who believes? Is this individual going down with the nation? Jesus gives great assurance to that individual also that the one who sees Jesus and believes, "I will not cast out."[10]

7. Conclusion

When Jesus spoke of choosing people in the Gospel of John, it was always in reference to an evangelistic mission, and a vocation to serve.

Even Judas was chosen to serve, if only in the sense that his betrayal was used by God to bring Jesus to the cross.

John's Gospel never speaks of individuals being chosen from all eternity for eternal life or death. As Forster and Marston summarized,

> All too often "election" has been viewed as an irresistible ticket to blessing, rather than as the bestowal of an office. Thus, for example, the words "You have not chosen me but I have chosen you" have been made into the assertion about God selecting who should be saved. This is unjustifiable, for the whole passage is addressed

---

[10] Ibid.

specifically to the apostles. The choice Jesus mentions is linked specifically to their "appointment," i.e., to apostolic office.[11]

---

[11] Roger T. Forster and V. Paul Marston, *God's Strategy in Human History* (Wheaton, IL: Tyndale House Publishers, Inc., 1974), 119-20.

12

Appointed to Eternal Life (Acts 13:48)

Be Prepared.
LORD BADEN POWELL

1. Introduction

"BUT THEN HOW CAN we be saved?"

The nine-year old boy nearly jumped out of the pew as he anxiously shouted the question. I could tell by the faces around him, that the other kids shared his concern.

It was the summer of 2005, and I was working as a summer camp chaplain.

Now, as you can imagine, not every kid was interested in what I had to say. Chapel was not the highlight of their day. They couldn't wait to play soccer, hike the trails, and go on the zip line. But some kids were interested, like that nine-year old boy. And it was fascinating to see how the different *groups* of kids would respond over the summer.

Some groups responded to my preaching. It seemed like there was a mini-revival at times! And then a new group would come in and it was a spiritual desert.

What made the difference, I wondered?

Why did some kids (and some groups of kids) respond, but not others?

The Bible tells us that one important factor is being prepared to hear the word of God. In Acts 13:48 we read,

> Now when the Gentiles heard this, they were glad and glorified the word of the Lord. *And as many as had been appointed to eternal life believed* (emphasis added).

Many think this verse means that God knew which Gentiles would believe, even before they were born.[1] But is that interpretation obvious?

Not to me.

I can't help but notice the passage is missing all of the words that might be used to support the traditional doctrine of election. That is, it

---

[1] For example, according to Arthur W. Pink, "Every artifice of human in-genuity has been employed to blunt the sharp edge of this scripture and to explain away the obvious meaning of these words, but it has been em-ployed in vain." In fact, according to Pink, even questioning the meaning of this passage was the sign of an unregenerate mind: "nothing will ever be able to reconcile this and similar passages to the mind of the natural man." In *The Sovereignty of God* (Grand Rapids, MI: Baker, 1969), p. 63

doesn't mention *election*, or *choice*, or *predestination*. It doesn't even mention *God*, or that He did the appointing! And yet some think this is one of the most obvious examples of God's predestining certain individuals to eternal life.

How come?

Everything hangs on the word "appointed." The English can give the impression that an outside power has chosen certain people to have eternal life. But what does the Greek actually mean?

2. What Does "Appointed" Mean?

The word for "appointed" is *tetagmenoi*, derived from *tassō*, which, as you might guess, has a range of meanings. Surprisingly, *none have to do with individual election to eternal life or death.*

Liddell and Scott point to its military use, "to arrange, put in order...esp. to draw up in order of battle, to form, array, marshal...to appoint to any service, military or civil...to appoint one to do a thing...to be appointed to do...to assign to a class...to place in a certain order..."[2]

Moulton and Milligan agree that *tetagmenoi* means to "put in its place," "appoint," and "enroll." For example, it was used for "those who had been appointed to the administration in the Serapeum."[3]

---

[2] Henry Liddell and Robert Scott, *An Intermediate Greek-English Lexicon* (Oxford: Clarendon, 1889, 1999), 793

[3] J. H. Moulton and G. Milligan, *Vocabulary of the Greek Testament* (Peabody, MA: Hendrickson, 1930, 2004), 626.

Likewise, BDAG gives *tassō* a vocational meaning, such as "to bring about an order of things by arranging."[4]

Isn't this odd?

If Luke had wanted to teach about God predestining individuals to eternal life, why use a word that, so far as the lexicons are concerned, is never used in Greek literature to teach that?

Why wouldn't Paul use one of the well-known words or phrases for election?

Or did he intend to teach something else?

Crucially, the lexicons tell us that *tetagmenoi* can also be translated in the middle voice. When taken that way, Moulton and Milligan say that *tassō* can mean "appoint for oneself" or "enter into an agreement with."[5] Likewise, BDAG says the middle can also mean, "devote oneself to a service" and to "belong to, to be classed among those possessing."[6]

In other words, it can mean that you have decided for yourself to do a certain service.

If we translate *tetagmenoi* in the middle voice, in a reflexive sense, in which the action is *done to oneself*, the verse could read:

---

[4] *Greek-English Lexicon of the New Testament and Other Early Christian Literature*, ed. Frederick William Danker, Third Edition (Chicago, IL: The University of Chicago Press, 2000), 991. Hereafter, BDAG.

[5] Moulton and Milligan, *Vocabulary*, 626.

[6] BDAG, 991.

As many *as were predisposed* to eternal life believed (Acts 13:48, emphasis added).

Or, David J. Williams offered this possible translation:

"as many as had set themselves [by their response to the Spirit's prompting] for eternal life became believers."[7]

Taken this way, Acts 13:48 means the Gentile believers *had predisposed themselves to eternal life* by being open to the truth. And that makes a great deal more sense in the context of Acts 13.

3. A Study in Contrasts

Acts 13 is a study in contrasts between people who are predisposed to hearing the truth and those who are not.

For example, at the beginning of the chapter (Acts 13:1-12), Luke tells the story of how Paul and Barnabas visited the island of Paphos where they met two men, a false prophet named Bar-Jesus, and a proconsul named Sergius Paulus.

The two men's attitudes toward the gospel couldn't have been more different.

On the one hand, Bar-Jesus is described in the most despicable terms. He is called deceitful, fraudulent, an enemy, a son of the devil, and

---

[7] David John Williams, *Acts* (Peabody, MA: Hendrickson, 1990), 239.

someone who deliberately perverts the way of the Lord (Acts 13:10). If anyone was predisposed to reject the truth, it was Bar-Jesus.

On the other hand, Luke goes out of his way to describe the proconsul as "an intelligent man." Unlike Bar-Jesus, he was concerned with the truth and was open to hear more (Acts 13:7).

All too predictably, the two men had very different reactions to Paul's gospel.

The proconsul "called for Barnabas and Saul and sought to hear the word of God" (Acts 13:7) and eventually believed (Acts 13:12), while Bar-Jesus, by contrast, rejected the apostles and "withstood them, seeking to turn the proconsul away from the faith" (Acts 13:7-8) and was cursed with blindness as a result (Acts 13:11).

Two very different men with two very different attitudes to the truth and to eternal life.

Later in the chapter, when Paul arrived in Pisidian Antioch, he began to preach in the local synagogue. Like the proconsul, some of the Jews, proselytes, and Gentiles were eager to hear more about Jesus, and they followed the apostles (Acts 13:42-43). But others, especially the Jews, were more like Bar-Jesus and "were filled with envy" at the city's positive response and "began contradicting the things spoken by Paul, and were blaspheming" (Acts 13:45). They rejected the message wholeheartedly, and didn't want the other Jews to hear or believe it!

Faced with this backlash, Paul made a dramatic announcement. He explained that their rejection of the gospel reflected their spiritual condition:

> "It was necessary that the word of God should be spoken to you first; but since you reject it, and *judge yourselves unworthy* of everlasting life, behold, we turn to the Gentiles" (Acts 13:46, emphasis added).

Why were they unworthy? Paul doesn't blame God's election for their unworthiness. In fact, election isn't raised as an issue at all in this chapter. Rather, Paul blames them. He points to their own agency. They did it to themselves. Instead of being open to the message of life, they were close-minded and instead of seeking the truth, they actively opposed it. And for that, they suffered the consequences. They missed out on eternal life.

4. The Contrast Between Acts 13:46 and 48

It is surely significant that Acts 13:46 and 13:48 are the only two verses in the whole of Acts that use the expression *everlasting life*. The fact that Luke places them so close together in the same chapter indicates they are antithetically parallel, meant to contrast with one another.[8]

---

[8] One difference is that v 46 is in the genitive, while v. 48 is in the accusative. Esther Yu L. Ng explains: "As for the alleged parallel/contrast

Compare the two verses:

"Since you repudiate it and *judge your-selves* unworthy of *eternal life*, behold, we are turning to the Gentiles" (Acts 13:46, NASB, emphasis added).

The reflexive translation of v 48 complements the self-condemnation of v 46:

As many *as were predisposed* to eternal life believed (Acts 13:48, emphasis added).

The Jews were closed to the truth, so they proved themselves unworthy of eternal life, while the Gentiles were hungry for the truth, predis-posed to it, so they believed the apostles' preach-ing.

Henry Alford agreed with this line of thought. He suggested that understanding *tetagmenoi* as an unconditional decree is forced, and that it would be better translated as *were disposed*, rather than *were appointed*:

---

between v 46 and v 48, it should be noted that the two verses have different grammatical constructions regarding 'eternal life' (ἄξιος with genitive τῆς αἰωνίου ζωῆς in v 46, versus ἦσαν τεταγμένοι with εἰς followed by accusative ζωὴν αἰώνιον in v 48). Thus the two construc-tions are not really parallels." See Esther Yue L. Ng, "ἦσαν τεταγμένοι in Acts 13:48: Middle Voice or Passive Voice?—Implications for the Doctrine of Divine Election," *CGST Journal* No. 50 (2011.1): 4-5. Avail-able online: https://www.cgst.edu/files/journal_content/mainpdf/125/J50_185_Art07.pdf. Accessed September 6, 2017.

48. [*tetagmenoi*] The meaning of this word must be determined by the context. The Jews had *judged themselves unworthy of eternal life* [v 46]; the Gentiles, as many as were disposed to eternal life [v 48], believed. *By whom* so disposed is not here declared; nor need the word be in this place further particularized. *We know that it is God who worketh in us the will to believe* and that the preparation of the heart is of Him; but to find *in this text* pre-ordination to life asserted is to force both the word and the context to a meaning which they do not contain.[9]

Similarly, A. T. Robertson agreed this verse speaks to the different dispositions of the Jews and the Gentiles:

The word "ordain" is not the best translation here. "Appointed," as Hackett shows, is better. The Jews here had voluntarily rejected the word of God. On the other side were those Gentiles who gladly accepted what the Jews had rejected, not all the Gentiles. Why these Gentiles here ranged themselves on God's side as opposed to the Jews Luke does not tell us. This verse

---

[9] Henry Alford, *The Greek Testament*, Vol. II: The Acts of the Apostles, The Epistles to the Romans and Corinthians, fifth edition (Cambridge: Deighton, Bell, and Co., 1865), 153, emphasis his.

does not solve the vexed problem of divine sovereignty and human free agency. There is no evidence that Luke had in mind an *absolutum decretum* of personal salvation.[10]

And finally, J. Vernon Bartlet said that Acts 13:48 conveyed the idea

"of preparedness of heart, without any thought as to how this came about… The best rendering then would be, 'were (found) disposed to eternal life,' which preserves the exact shade of the verb ('to set in order, arrange, dispose') and has just that degree of ambiguity which belongs to the original."[11]

5. Conclusion

Although some interpreters think Acts 13:48 is a home-run for individual election to eternal life, that isn't Paul's point at all.

In keeping with the rest of chapter 13, Luke wants us to recognize the different ways people prepare themselves to be open to God's truth or not. You can either be like Bar-Jesus or the

---

[10] A. T. Robertson, *Word Pictures in the New Testament*. Emphasis his. See http://www.biblestudytools.com/commentaries/robertsons-word-pictures/acts/acts-13-48.html. Accessed September 7, 2017.
[11] J. Vernon Bartlet, *The New Century Bible: The Acts*, quoted in Shank, *Elect*, 187.

proconsul; either like the Jews, or the Gentiles; either open to the truth or closed to it.

Depending on your attitude, you can either judge yourself unworthy of eternal life, or be disposed to it.

In sum, Acts 13:48 isn't about God's choosing some individuals to believe and passing over everyone else. It's about every individual's responsibility to prepare himself to hear the truth, to seek it out, and when he hears, to believe it.

How is your heart?

13

The Golden Chain
(Romans 8:29-30)

As children we recognized that we belonged to an unusual, even exceptional, family, but the effect was different on each of us.
DAVID ROCKEFELLER

1. Introduction

HAVE YOU EVER NOTICED how many rich kids go bad? They're born with unimaginable opportunities. But with great wealth comes great temptations, and the children of the rich often self-destruct. As Erika Brown reported, there is a whole industry devoted to rehabilitating wealthy children:

> Outsourcing the problem kids of the wealthy is a booming business. Each year 10,000 kids attend residential programs to

161

get off drugs and deal with emotional and
psychological problems. Fixing bad kids is
a $2 billion-a-year industry in the private
sector.[1]

Like the children of the rich, believers have
been given every advantage to "reign in life" (Rom
5:17). But sadly, too many Christians fall to temp-
tation and fail to mature.

Of all the verses that have traditionally been
used to teach that God elects individuals to eternal life, Rom 8:29-30 may be the most formidable.
Scholars call it *the golden chain.*

The traditional interpretation says that God
chose some individuals to have eternal life, and
they will unconditionally progress from being
declared righteous (justified) to being physically
glorified in the resurrection of the dead.

By contrast, I will argue each of those terms
must be rethought in light of the fact that it is
the conclusion to Paul's treatise on sanctification
(Romans 5-8) in which he explained the entirely
conditional nature of spiritual growth culminating
in ruling with Christ.

---

[1] Erika Brown, "When Rich Kids Go Bad," *Forbes* (10/14/2002). See
http://www.forbes.com/forbes/2002/1014/140.html. Accessed July 10,
2017.

2. How to Be Sanctified

In Rom 8:1-38, Paul answers the question of how the Christian can overcome the experience of bondage described in chapter 7. He says:

> There is therefore now no servitude to sin for those who are in Christ Jesus, who do not walk according to the flesh, but according to the Spirit (Rom 8:1, Hodges Translation[2]).

In order for a believer not to experience servitude to sin, two things must happen.

First, you must be *in Christ Jesus*. That is, the foundation of your escape from bondage is found in your union with Christ. This happens when you first believe in Christ for eternal life and become regenerate.

Second, you must not walk according to *the flesh* but according to *the Spirit* (Rom 8:1). The key to sanctification is to develop a spiritual mindset. Focusing on the law led Paul into defeat. Instead, he needed to set his mind on the things of the Spirit:

> For those who live according to the flesh set their minds on the things of the flesh, but those who live according to the Spirit, the things of the Spirit (Rom 8:5).

---

[2] This translation is from Zane C. Hodges, *Romans: Deliverance from Wrath* (Corinth, TX: Grace Evangelical Society, 2013).

If you set your mind on the Spirit, He can give life to your dead bodies (Rom 8:11), enabling you to put the deeds of the body to death and really live (Rom 8:12-13).

However, as Paul's experience in Romans 7 demonstrated, that victory isn't inevitable. Paul could have stayed trapped in a legalistic mindset, as could any Christian. Think of how popular legalism is as a method of sanctification in Catholic and Orthodox churches, for example. If you stay trapped in legalism, you'll stay a debtor to the flesh and stuck in the agonizing situation Paul was left in in Rom 7:24.

In other words, for Paul, sanctification is conditional. Not every believer will move from servitude to sin to practical righteousness, but God has a special destiny for those who do.

Christians who walk according to the Spirit and grow to spiritual maturity are God's "sons" (Rom 8:14) and will be co-heirs with Christ (Rom 8:17).

But aren't we all God's sons and heirs?

Not quite.

In Gal 4:1-7, Paul distinguished between *small children* and mature *sons,* and that seems to be what Paul is referring to here. These represent two different levels of spiritual maturity. If we have set our minds on the things of the Spirit and not on the things of the flesh, we won't be immature children but God's mature sons.

The idea of sonship is especially important because of its relationship to inheritance, a topic we have already explored in the context of vocational election and rewards. As James D. G. Dunn explains,

> Not least of importance in the concept of sonship is the fact that it links into the theme of inheritance, not unnaturally since the primary purpose of adoption was to provide a suitable heir.[3]

That's why Paul goes on to distinguish between two kinds of heirs with two kinds of inheritances. On the one hand, there are "heirs of God" (Rom 8:17a), which applies to all believers. On the other hand, there are those who suffer with Christ and become "joint-heirs with Christ" (Rom 8:17b).

The two should not be confused. As Colin Kruse explains:

> To be "heirs of God" means to be those to whom God will give an inheritance. To be "co-heir with Christ" means to be those who share the inheritance God gives to Christ."[4]

---

[3] James D. G. Dunn, *Romans 1-8* (Grand Rapids, MI: Zondervan, 2015), 462.
[4] Colin G. Kruse, *Paul's Letter to the Romans* (Grand Rapids, MI: Eerdmans, 2012), 340.

Being a co-heir with Christ involves a greater inheritance because as the Firstborn (8:29), Christ receives a greater inheritance than others. Hence, Paul is saying that while all believers will have an inheritance as "heirs of God," there is a special inheritance reserved for overcomers.

3. Do All Things Lead to Good for Everyone?

The conditional nature of becoming practically righteous and spiritually mature puts this promise in a different light:

> And we know that all things work to-
> gether for good to those who love God,
> to those who are the called according
> to His purpose (Rom 8:28)

Many think this is an unqualified promise to all believers. They think it means that no matter how you live—whether you are faithful to Christ or not—everything in your life will turn out for good in the end.

That's wrong. Very wrong. As David Jeremiah explains,

> Romans 8:28 is not a promise that's the
> equivalent of the world saying, "Don't
> worry—it'll all work out." This is a condi-
> tional promise given for people who have

met two conditions: They love God and have been called by God.[5]

First of all, the promise of Rom 8:28 is given to Christians *who love God*. Some interpreters think that is just shorthand for "Christian." All believers love God, they say. But it's hard to accept that interpretation, given Paul's extensive argument in Romans 5-8 that not all Christians will be equally sanctified or follow the Spirit. Not every Christian loves God any more than every Israelite loved God. That's why Jude said, "keep yourselves in the love of God" (Jude 21). Loving God is not guaranteed.

In other words, contrary to what some commentators say, "those who love God" is not a generic term for all Christians, but only refers to those who actually do love God.

Second, the promise is to those Christians who are *called according to His purpose*.

Once again, some interpreters simply take this as shorthand for all believers.[6] But can anyone who has read the Bible think that all of God's people fulfill God's calling for them?

Absolutely not.

As we saw in previous chapters, individual Israelites, as well as whole generations, failed in

[5] David Jeremiah, *Captured by Grace: No One Is Beyond the Reach of Loving God* (Nashville, TN: Thomas Nelson, 2006), 97.
[6] Douglas J. Moo, *The Epistle to the Romans* (Grand Rapids, MI: Eerdmans, 1996), 530.

their respective calling (as Paul will go on to discuss in Romans 9-11). The same is true of Christians (e.g., think of the carnal Corinthians).

Hence, while many interpret Rom 8:28 as an unconditional promise made to all Christians, I believe it is best understood as a conditional promise made to believers who love God and seek to obey Him.

Understanding the conditional nature of Romans 5-8 puts the "golden chain" of Rom 8:29-30 in a different light.

4. The Golden Chain

I suggest to you that the "golden chain" does not describe something that is true of all believers, but rather completes Paul's thought about the special glory God will give to overcomers. Each link in the chain needs to be rethought in light of that context.

A. Foreknown

The "golden chain" opens with God's foreknowledge (Rom 8:29). The concept of foreknowledge has taken on much theological and philosophical baggage over the centuries, and it is hard to read Rom 8:29 without assuming those controversies.

However, the word for *foreknowledge* appears seven times as a verb (Acts 26:5; Rom 8:29; 11:2;

1 Pet 1:20; and 2 Pet 3:17) and twice as a noun (Acts 2:23; 1 Pet 1:2). It means "to know beforehand or in advance" or to "choose beforehand" (BDAG, 866). That is not quite as majestic or as mysterious as theological tradition would suggest.

Indeed, as you can see from the references, the Biblical concept of *foreknowledge* is not necessarily related to divine omniscience at all. *Humans have foreknowledge, too.* Hence, Paul spoke about people who "knew from the first" about him and his time as a Pharisee (Acts 26:5). And Peter told his readers that they already knew [*proginōskontes*] to avoid heresies about the Day of the Lord (2 Pet 3:17). Neither of these uses refers to eternal knowledge or to divine omniscience. It simply means that Paul and Peter's audiences had knowledge prior to the time they were writing.

Similarly, Rom 8:29 means that God already knew what would happen to everyone who loved Him and who followed their calling. They would be *conformed*.

B. Conformed

In Rom 8:29 we read that overcomers will be "conformed to the image of His Son, so that He would be the firstborn among many brethren." What kind of conformity is that?

This is not a general statement about eternal salvation. The "golden chain" is often interpreted that way, but Paul has something else in mind.

The clue is when Paul says this conformity has to do with Jesus' status as the "firstborn." As we saw earlier, being the firstborn is an inheritance concept. That tells us this conformity is kingdom related and rewards related.

Remember that, in Rom 8:17, Paul distinguished between two kinds of inheritances. There is being "heirs of God" which is true of all believers. But there is a second heirship, i.e., being "fellow heirs with Christ." As the Firstborn, Christ has a special inheritance from God. He gets the double portion. But Jesus will share that double portion with believers who have suffered for Him. All believers are heirs of God, because faith is the only condition. But Paul says that being a co-heir with Christ also depends on whether "we suffer with Him."

If you are a believer who has suffered for Christ, you will be a co-heir, too, and will share in His double-portion inheritance. Jesus will be glorified. And when He is, you will be "be glorified together" with Him with that special reward.

In sum, when Paul speaks about "conformity," it is not a reference to eternal salvation in general, but refers to ruling with Christ in His special status as the Firstborn.

C. Predetermined

The word *predestined* is loaded with theological and philosophical baggage, but the word *proorizō* simply means *to decide beforehand*. It doesn't necessarily evoke timeless foreknowledge (see Appendix 2). In fact, since there is no "before" or "after" in timeless eternity, a decision "beforehand" strongly suggests a decision *within time*.[7]

In any case, Paul is saying that God has already decided how to reward faithful Christians who love Him.

D. Called

The overcomers are also "called." As Zane Hodges explains, citing BDAG, in this case "called" has the extended meaning of "choose for receipt of a special benefit or experience, call."[8] Faithful believers who suffer with Christ in this life will be chosen to receive the special benefit of ruling as a co-heir with Christ in the next one.

E. Vindicated

The next link in the golden chain is "justification," which many automatically take to mean forensic justification. But Paul also used that word

---

[7] For a Biblical and philosophical argument that God is in time see Nicholas Wolterstoff, "God Everlasting," *Contemporary Philosophy of Religion*, ed. Steven M Cahn and David Shatz (New York, NY: Oxford University Press, 1982), 77-98. For a defense of God being timeless without creation and temporal subsequent to creation see William Lane Craig, "God, Time, and Eternity," available at http://www.reasonablefaith.org/god-time-and-eternity#ixzz4s6pWxEbs. Accessed Sept 9, 2017.
[8] Hodges, *Romans*, 240.

in the sense of *vindication*. In 1 Tim 3:16, Paul says that Jesus was "justified [vindicated] in the Spirit." That doesn't mean Jesus was declared righteous on the basis of faith in Himself apart from works. It means Jesus' mission was vindicated by the Holy Spirit at His baptism (Matt 3:15-17), transfiguration (Matt 17:5), and resurrection (Rom 1:3, 4).[9]

Likewise, I believe Paul's use of justification in Rom 8:30 should be understood as *vindication*. God has decided beforehand that faithful Christians who love Him, and who suffer for Christ while pursuing their calling from Him, will be vindicated at the Judgment Seat of Christ and rewarded with ruling with Christ as His co-heirs (cf. 1 Cor 3:11-15).

F. Glorified

The end of the "golden chain" is *glorification*. I believe this is a special glorification, conditioned on being an overcomer.

Commenting on Rom 8:15-17, Ernest Kasemann suggested that something like this was the case:

> Only he who participates on earth in the passion of the *kyrios* will participate in his glory. As in 2 Cor 13:4, suffering with him

---

[9] William MacDonald, *Believer's Bible Commentary,* ed. Art Farstad (Nashville, TN: Thomas Nelson, 1995), 2090.

is the paradoxical guarantee of sharing the *basileia*. *Eiper* might well refer to the reality of the standing and experiences of the Christian. But the final sentence which follows and the sharp break in thought more naturally suggests a hortatory and conditional understanding which directs us back to vv 12f. Only those who resist the flesh with suffering can overcome.[10]

Likewise, Zane Hodges agrees this is a special, conditional, glorification for overcomers: "When He is glorified as the Ruler of all creation, they will be co-glorified *together with Him* sharing the same rulership."[11]

Glorification is not the general glorification that will be experienced by all believers in their new bodies, but here refers to receiving the special glory of receiving the reward of ruling with Christ.

5. Conclusion

When dealing with election, the "golden chain" of Rom 8:29-30 is one of the most difficult passages to read with fresh eyes. Every element of the verse carries centuries of theological baggage, and must be rethought in proper context.

---

[10] Ernst Kasemann, *Commentary on Romans*, trans by Geoffrey Bromily (Grand Rapids, MI: Eerdmans, 1980), 229.

[11] Hodges, *Romans*, 243.

Once you see the "golden chain" comes at the conclusion of Paul's treatise on sanctification in Romans 5-8, you realize that it is not an unconditional statement about God's choosing some individuals to be saved, but a conditional promise that Christians who have fulfilled their calling, will be vindicated before God and rewarded by sharing in Christ's own glory through ruling with Him in His kingdom.

14

Everybody Hates Esau
(Romans 9:13)

There aren't a lot of ironclad rules of family life, but here's one: No matter how much your parents deny it—and here's betting they deny it a lot—they have a favorite child. And if you're a parent, so do you.
JEFFREY KLUGER

1. Introduction

WHO WAS THE FAVORITE child in your family? Every family has one. You know it. I know it.

Sometimes it's a status held by one child. Sometimes it changes, as different children can be the favorite child at different times. As Dr. Ellen Libby explains,

> Favorite child status can be handed off from child to child at different time

periods. Optimally, all children in all families experience the status of being the favorite child and benefit from the advantages coming with that position. Mothers may prefer infants, and all children are favored when they are infants. Fathers may prefer adolescents, favoring the child passing through this stage. In some families, who is favored frequently changes, reflecting the fluid interests and needs of the parents.[1]

Here's a thought: *even God's family has a favorite child.* And what's more, that favorite child has changed over time. Grasping that helps us to decipher Paul's statement about Jacob and Esau in Rom 9:13.

Although traditional interpretations of Paul have seen in that passage individual election to eternal life, Paul was really talking about God's prerogative to choose which nations should serve Him.

2. Everybody Hates Esau (Rom 9:13)

Many interpreters take the story of God's choice of Jacob over Esau as an example of

---

[1] Ellen Libby, "The Favorite Child: Unraveling This Pervasive Dynamic," *The Huffington Post* (05/25/2010). See http://www.huffingtonpost.com/dr-ellen-libby/the-favorite-child-unrave_b_512154.html

individual predestination to eternal life and death. Here is the verse:

> Just as it is written, "Jacob I loved, but Esau I hated." What shall we say then? There is no injustice with God, is there? May it never be! For He says to Moses, "I will have mercy on whom I have mercy, and I will have compassion on whom I have compassion" (Rom 9:13-15).

"Jacob I have loved" is supposed to mean that God individually elected Jacob to eternal life.

"Esau I have hated" is supposed to mean that God individually elected him to eternal death (or, at least, not to eternal life).

And "I will have mercy on whom I have mercy" is taken to justify the seeming arbitrariness of individual election to eternal life or death.

But that's not at all what is meant by that passage. The clue should have come from v 12, which is not often quoted:

> It was said to her, "The older will serve the younger" (Rom 9:12).

This is about election to service, not to eternal life.

3. Chosen to Be Ancestors of Messiah

Before mentioning Jacob and Esau in v 13, Paul used the example of Ishmael and Isaac in vv 7-8.

You remember that Ishmael was Abraham's first son, but not the son promised by God. That privilege fell to the son Abraham had with Sarah, whom he named Isaac.

And why was Isaac, the second child, chosen? What was he chosen *for*? Was he individually pre-destined for eternal life?

No. Rather, Isaac was chosen to be *one of the ancestors of the Messiah*, the promised Seed (Gal 3:16). This was an election for service. There was a mission to accomplish, and it would be accomplished through Isaac.

When, in vv 10-13, Paul switched examples to God's choice of Jacob over Esau, he had the same vocational election in mind. Jacob and Esau were both Abraham's sons, but God chose Jacob, not Esau, to be *the Messiah's ancestor*.

Again, this is a thoroughly vocational election, not an individual election to eternal life. As Jonathan Grothe notes,

> He selected (in accord with his plan) Isaac instead of Ishmael, Jacob over Esau. This *selection* to be the bearer of the promised Seed, this *selection* to fulfill a part in the historical unfolding of the plan, must be

kept distinct from *election* to eternal salvation.[2]

4. Jacob and Esau Represent Nations

Not only is the choice of Jacob and Esau *vocational*, it is also *corporate*.

Although the prophecy said, "The older shall serve the younger" (Rom 9:12), individually speaking, Esau never served Jacob. In fact, the reverse was true. It was Jacob who bowed down to Esau, addressed him as "Lord" and called himself Esau's servant (Gen 33:3, 5, 8, 13).[3]

Then how was this verse fulfilled?

Corporately.

Paul's point was that Jacob and Esau were chosen as representative heads of two *nations*, namely, Israel and the Edomites:

> And the Lord said to her: "Two *nations* are in your womb, two *peoples* shall be separated from your body; one people shall be stronger than the other, and *the older shall serve the younger*" (Gen 25:23, emphasis added).

---

[2] Jonathan F. Grothe, *The Justification of the Ungodly: An Interpretation of Romans*, Second Edition (St. Catharines, ON: N.P., 2012), 400-401.

[3] Roger T. Forster and V. Paul Marston, *God's Strategy in Human History* (Wheaton, IL: Tyndale, 1974), 59.

The corporate meaning of God's choice of Jacob over Esau is also clear when you look at the passage that Paul quotes from Malachi 1,

> "I have loved you," says the Lord.
> "Yet you say, 'In what way have You loved us?'
> Was not Esau Jacob's brother?"
> Says the Lord.
> "*Yet Jacob I have loved*;
> *But Esau I have hated*,
> And laid waste his mountains and his heritage
> For the jackals of the wilderness."
> Even though Edom has said,
> "We have been impoverished,
> But we will return and build the desolate places,"
> Thus says the Lord of hosts:
> "They may build, but I will throw down;
> They shall be called the Territory of Wickedness,
> And the people against whom
> the Lord will have indignation forever.
> Your eyes shall see,
> And you shall say,
> 'The Lord is magnified beyond the border of Israel'" (Mal 1:2-5, emphasis added).

This prophecy was given centuries after Jacob and Esau the individuals had died. It was not about them as individuals, but about the *nations* they represented—Israel and Edom.

It was about God's leniency towards Israel, as compared to His harsh judgment of the Edomites.

You may know the two nations had a troubled history.

After the Exodus, the king of Edom refused to let Israel enter the Promised Land (Num 20:14-21; Judg 11:17). Consequently, the Israelites travelled around Edom, going through the wilderness (Num 21:4; Judg 11:18). Despite this bad treatment, God told the Israelites not to detest the Edomites (Deut 23:7-8) because they were related.

Eventually, King Saul and King David went to war with the Edomites and subdued them (1 Sam 14:47-48; 2 Sam 8:13-14). While King David achieved dominance over Edom during his reign, they rebelled under Solomon (1 Kgs 11:14-22), only to be subjected again under King Jehosphat (1 Kgs 22:47-50). And the Edomites were defeated again by King Amaziah (2 Chron 25:11-12).

Esau did, indeed, serve Jacob.

5. Conclusion

In quoting Malachi, Paul was not thereby teaching individual election to eternal life or death. He was pointing to God's favor towards Israel over the Edomites. As Forster and Marston recognize, "God's 'love of Jacob but hatred of Esau' means this: God has chosen to give to the nation of Israel a special place and privileged position."[4]

Why make this point?

When the Jews of Paul's day objected to God's turning to the Gentiles to serve His purposes, Paul pointed to this passage in Malachi to show that God is free to have mercy and compassion on whichever nations He wants (Rom 9:15). That is how God has always acted.

Whether or not Jacob and Esau were individually elected to eternal life or death is completely beside Paul's point.

---

[4] Ibid., 61.

15

Pharaoh's Heart
(Romans 9:17)

Men are disturbed not by things,
but by the view which they take of them.
EPICTETUS

1. Introduction

I USED TO THINK I was a very calm, even-keeled kind of person. Nothing could upset me. I was Stoical.

Then I had kids. Three of them. All under four. And it turned out I had anger issues!

The ancient Stoics believed that people and circumstances were not the real cause of your emotional disturbances. Albert Ellis developed his Rational Emotive Behavior Therapy based on that insight. The real cause of our emotional disturbances are not the circumstances themselves, but what we *think* about those circumstances, especially when that thinking is *irrational*.

When God told Pharaoh to let the Jews go, he refused. When God insisted, Pharaoh got mad. He irrationally thought he could defy God. He was wrong.

When Paul mentioned Pharaoh in Rom 9:17, some mistakenly take it as a case of individual predestination to damnation. But remember that Paul was answering a Jewish objection to his gospel—how can God still be considered faithful to Israel if He has turned to the Gentiles? What about all the promises and covenants God has made with Israel? Has the word of God become ineffective? (Rom 9:6).

Paul's response was to argue that it is God's prerogative to choose which nations will serve His purposes, whether Israel or the Gentiles. That prerogative was evident in His choice of Israel over Edom.

That raised another objection. Is it unjust for God to act that way? (Rom 9:14).

Absolutely not.

> What shall we say then? There is no injustice with God, is there? May it never be! For He says to Moses, "I will have mercy on whom I have mercy, and I will have compassion on whom I have compassion." So then it does not depend on the man who wills or the man who runs, but

on God who has mercy. For the Scripture
says to Pharaoh, "For this very purpose I
raised you up, to demonstrate My power
in you, and that My name might be proclaimed throughout the whole earth." So
then He has mercy on whom He desires,
and He hardens whom He desires (Rom
9:14-18).

This passage has been used to prove that God
chooses some individuals for eternal life, and pur-
posefully hardens others so they will be damned
forever, and somehow that displays God's power
and mercy.

On the contrary, Paul was still defending God's
prerogative to choose which nations will serve His
purposes. It is about corporate election to service,
not individual election to eternal life.

2. Pharaoh Could Have Been Used for Good

If you look at Genesis and Exodus, you find
different Pharaohs reacted differently to God's
purposes.

The Pharaoh of Joseph's day was used to *bless*
the Jewish people by saving them during a time of
famine.

The Pharaoh of Moses' youth hardened his
heart against God and tried to *kill* the first born
sons of the Hebrews.

And the Pharaoh of the Exodus similarly abused the Hebrew slaves and refused to let them go.

The Exodus Pharaoh—who represented Egypt—could have been a vessel for honor, as some of his predecessors were. He could have served God's purposes by letting Israel go peacefully, being a blessing to them. Instead, he became a vessel for dishonor. But even a dishonorable vessel serves a purpose.[1] So would Egypt. Despite himself, Pharaoh let Israel go free.

However, because of their rebellion, because of their refusal to serve God, both Pharaoh and Egypt became fit for destruction.[2] As the servants of Pharaoh warned him,

> How long shall this man be a snare to us?
> Let the men go, that they may serve the
> Lord their God. *Do you not yet know that
> Egypt is destroyed*? (Exod 10:8, emphasis
> added, LXX).

The destruction here is *temporal*, not *eternal*. This was a question of physical and political punishment for failing to serve God by not immediately releasing the Israelites.[3] Eternal life and death are not in view.

---

[1] J. D. Myers, *The Re-Justification of God: An Exegetical and Theological Study of Romans 9:10-24* (Dallas, OR: Redeeming Press, 2015), 62-63.
[2] These were different Pharaohs, but the attitude was the same.
[3] Zane C. Hodges, *Romans: Deliverance from Wrath* (Corinth, TX: Grace Evangelical Society, 2013), 272.

3. Jeremiah's Potter

Paul anticipated an objection to his illustration. Why does God find fault, if even a disobedient nation serves His purposes?

In answer, Paul compared God's use of Pharaoh to a potter working with clay (Rom 9:20-23), an analogy likely taken from Jer 18:1-13. Although many take this as the quintessential illustration of unconditional individual election to eternal life, once again, the point of Jeremiah's illustration is clearly vocational.

In that passage, Jeremiah warned Israel that God was free to raise up or to tear down nations at His pleasure. I will put all the corporate terms in italics so you don't miss them:

> Then the word of the Lord came to me saying, "Can I not, *O house of Israel*, deal with you as this potter does?" declares the Lord. "Behold, like the clay in the potter's hand, so are you in My hand, *O house of Israel*. At one moment I might speak concerning a *nation* or concerning a *kingdom* to uproot, to pull down, or to destroy it; if that *nation* against which I have spoken turns from its evil, I will relent concerning the calamity I planned to bring on it. Or at another moment I might speak concerning a *nation* or concerning a *kingdom* to build up or to plant it; if it does evil in My

sight by not obeying My voice, then I will think better of the good with which I had promised to bless it. So now then, speak to *the men of Judah* and against *the inhabitants of Jerusalem* saying, 'Thus says the Lord, "Behold, I am fashioning calamity against you and devising a plan against you. Oh turn back, each of you from his evil way, and reform your ways and your deeds."' But they will say, 'It's hopeless! For we are going to follow our own plans, and each of us will act according to the stubbornness of his evil heart.'

"Therefore thus says the Lord, 'Ask now among the *nations*, Who ever heard the like of this? The virgin of Israel Has done a most appalling thing'" (Jer 18:1-13, emphasis added).

"Israel." "Nation." "Kingdom." "Men of Judah." "Inhabitants of Jerusalem." This passage is thoroughly corporate, not individualistic. And it concerns temporal destinies, not eternal ones.

According to Jeremiah, the image of the potter and the clay illustrates how God may choose a nation for blessing or for destruction. The outcome depends on their response to Him. If a chosen nation rebels against God, then He will destroy it. And if a nation chosen for destruction suddenly turns from its evil, then God won't destroy it, even though that was His original intention. God is responsive and just. If we change our actions, He'll change His. If the clay shifts, God will adapt and have His way, either way.

Was that Paul's answer to the question over how could God still find fault?

Jeremiah's point, and Paul's too, is that God is not unjust because His preference is for people to obey. But if they rebel, He'll use that for His own purposes, while still holding them accountable for their rebellion.

Imagine if you were thinking of buying a new laptop when someone decides to steal it from you. Wouldn't it be just to use the insurance money to buy the new laptop you wanted, while still holding the thief accountable? Of course.

Likewise, it is perfectly just for God to use Egypt's rebellion for His purposes and still hold them accountable for their sin.

4. That Makes Me Mad!

I would like to make a comment about the verses that speak of Pharaoh's hardened heart.

Some verses say that Pharaoh hardened his own heart (Exod 8:15, 32; 9:34). Others say that God did it (Exod 7:3; 9:12; 10:1, 20, 27; 11:10; 14:4, 8). Theologians have long debated the philosophical implications of God being in control versus man being free.

I think that may be over-thinking the text.

Has anyone ever made you angry?

Maybe someone cheated you at work, or cut you off in traffic, or harmed someone you loved. We say, "That makes me angry!" But what do we mean by that?

We don't literally mean the other person "makes" us angry by controlling our emotions the way a pilot flies an airplane or a computer programmer programs a machine.

It's an expression that means we do not like what's going on.

When the Bible says that God hardened Pharaoh's heart, it's not making a mysterious philosophical statement. Its saying that God's good plans for Israel made Pharaoh mad. God knew that, and He did it anyway.

Moreover, Pharaoh was an illustration of how God often punishes the disobedient by giving them over to their own wicked desires (Ps 81:12; Acts 7:42; Rom 1:24). Rather than strive with Pharaoh any longer, God left him to his own desires and used that to fulfill His purposes for Israel.

For Paul, it seemed that Israel was going through a similar experience. Her heart was hardened against the Messiah, so God turned to the Gentiles.

5. God Used Cyrus

That wasn't easy for the Jews to hear, especially those who believed in divine determinism. Paul imagines an objector wondering how anyone can be responsible for their actions since no one can resist God's will (Rom 9:19)? The Jewish objector is implying that by rejecting the Messiah the Jews were only doing what God willed for them to do, and should not be blamed for it. Since God determines everything, they had no other choice. Ironically, many Christians, especially Calvinists, assume the objector is right to be deterministic. As Jeremy Myers notes,

> I often find it interesting when Calvinists quote Rom 9:19 to defend their position, for in so doing, they are actually quoting a person who objects to what Paul teaches. It is not Paul, but the person who objects to Paul's argument, who believes that nobody can resist God's will.[4]

The question is—did Paul share that theology? Was Paul deterministic like that? Myers, for one, does not think so, and I am liable to agree,

> The fact that Paul seeks to refute an imaginary objector who believes that no one can resist God's will, means that Paul himself believes that people can *and do*

---

[4] Myers, *The Re-Justification of God*, 58.

resist God's will. Exhibit 1, for Paul, is the objector himself.[5]

Paul's reply in v 20 was to allude to Isaiah 45 which tells the story of Cyrus, another world leader whom God chose for service[6]:

> "Thus says the Lord to His anointed,
> To Cyrus, whose right hand I have held—
> To subdue nations before him
> And loose the armor of kings,
> To open before him the double doors,
> So that the gates will not be shut" (Isa 45:1).

God gave Cyrus the victory over other nations and later used him to allow the exiled Jews to return to Israel from Babylon.[7] Cyrus, like Pharaoh, became a serving vessel for God.

However, Israel wasn't pleased with God's choice of Cyrus. How could God abandon Israel and use the Gentiles to serve Him? Here is God's response:

> "Woe to him who strives with his Maker!
> Let the potsherd strive with the potsherds of the earth!
> Shall the clay say to him who forms it,

---

[5] Ibid., 59. Emphasis his.

[6] Tom Holland, *Romans: The Divine Marriage* (Eugene, OR: Pickwick, 2011), 329.

[7] William MacDonald, *Believer's Bible Commentary*, ed. Art Farstad (Dallas, TX: Thomas Nelson, 1995), 973.

'What are you making?'
Or shall your handiwork say, 'He has no
hands'?" (Isa 45:9).

This is Paul's point against the objector in v 20.
You'll notice the context doesn't deal with individual election to eternal life, but with corporate
election to a vocation.

Isaiah's lesson was the same as Jeremiah's,
which was the same as Paul's. *God has the prerogative to use whatever nations or individuals He
wants to achieve His purposes.* Seeing that Israel
hardened themselves against the Messiah, God
was perfectly free to change serving vessels and
turn His attention towards the Gentiles to accomplish His purposes.

6. Conclusion

Read over Romans 9 again. See if you can
notice Paul's emphasis on nations and corporate
people.

Although the Jews objected to Paul's claim that
God was working with the Gentiles, Paul showed
that God has always had the prerogative to choose
which nations will serve His purposes. Instead
of questioning God's prerogative, we should ask
ourselves whether we're serving Him through our
obedience or our disobedience. Anything other
than obedience would be irrational.

16

The Remnant
(Romans 11:5-7)

Why fit in when you were born to stand out!
DR. SEUSS

1. Introduction

THE CITY WHERE I grew up was so secular, I didn't even know Who Jesus was.

For example, in elementary school, I remember our teacher telling us that some knights were going to visit the class. I was so excited! Real knights! Imagine my disappointment when some old men in berets walked in handing out necklaces with a wooden plus sign. (FYI, they were Catholic Knights of Columbus.) I thought, "Wow, these guys sure love math!"

I might have been told about Jesus at some point in my life. If so, I do not remember it.

So when I heard the gospel as a teenager, and believed in Jesus, I found myself belonging to a very small faith community. Less than 1% of the population of Quebec is Evangelical. It was quite lonely. It's hard not to wonder—am I the only sane person left?

Likewise, most Jews in Paul's day rejected Jesus as the Messiah. When God then turned to preach the gospel to the Gentiles, the Jewish believers were left wondering—was all of Israel lost?

In response, Paul assured them there was a remnant chosen by grace.

2. A Chosen Remnant

Here's what Paul says:

> In the same way then, there has also come to be at the present time *a remnant according to God's gracious choice*. But if it is by grace, it is no longer on the basis of works, otherwise grace is no longer grace. What then? What Israel is seeking, it has not obtained, but those who were chosen obtained it, *and the rest were hardened* (Rom 11:5-7, emphasis added).

Many interpret Paul to mean there are individuals that God predestined from all eternity to believe, and He chose others to be damned.

Once again, the context suggests a simpler interpretation.

While most Jews did harden themselves against believing in the Messiah, there was a remnant who believed. That is, they became a remnant, not by God's timelesslessly eternal choice of some individuals to eternal life, but because they believed by faith alone, in Christ alone.

3. Bowing to Baal

Paul preceded his argument with an episode from the life of Elijah who complained to God about Israel's apostasy:

> I say then, has God cast away His people? Certainly not! For I also am an Israelite, of the seed of Abraham, of the tribe of Benjamin. God has not cast away His people whom He foreknew. Or do you not know what the Scripture says of Elijah, how he pleads with God against Israel, saying, "Lord, they have killed Your prophets and torn down Your altars, and I alone am left, and they seek my life"? But what does the divine response say to him? "I have reserved for Myself seven thousand men who have not bowed the knee to Baal" (Rom 11:1-4).

The quote about God reserving men for Himself comes from 1 Kgs 19:15-18:

> Then the Lord said to him: "Go, return on your way to the Wilderness of Damascus; and when you arrive, anoint Hazael as king over Syria. Also you shall anoint Jehu the son of Nimshi as king over Israel. And Elisha the son of Shaphat of Abel Meholah you shall anoint as prophet in your place. It shall be that whoever escapes the sword of Hazael, Jehu will kill; and whoever escapes the sword of Jehu, Elisha will kill. *Yet I have reserved seven thousand in Israel, all whose knees have not bowed to Baal, and every mouth that has not kissed him*" (emphasis added).

Elijah thought he was the only faithful Israelite left, but God assured him there were others. Seven thousand, in fact.

Why were they "reserved" by God?

Not because God had predestined them individually to eternal life, but because they hadn't "bowed the knee to Baal."

In other words, *they did something* that made them stand out from the crowd. They refused to worship Baal. That made them a remnant.

4. Chosen by Grace

Likewise, Paul assured the Romans that God still had a remnant in Israel. Paul said this remnant was chosen by grace, not by works. Does that mean they were predestined?

No.

"Chosen by grace" is Paul's shorthand for the doctrine of justification. As he says in Rom 4:6a: "Therefore it is of faith that it might be according to grace."

Something being "according to grace" means it is apart from works.

In other words, the remnant was chosen according to grace because they believed in Christ for salvation, *apart from works.*[1]

Romans 11:5-7 doesn't teach individual election to eternal life. It teaches us about the importance of the doctrine of justification by faith apart from works and how that is the criteria for being part of the remnant in an apostate world.

5. Conclusion

In Romans 9-11 in general, or in Rom 11:5-7 in particular, Paul was not making a point about God's choosing individuals for eternal life or death. He was clarifying God's plans for Israel. He

---

[1] Laurence M. Vance, *The Other Side of Calvinism* (Revised Edition) (Pensacola, FL: Vance Publications, 2007), 371-73; Forster and Marston, *God's Strategy*, 128.

argued that Israel's rejection of the Messiah was not a sign of God's unfaithfulness to them, but of Israel's unfaithfulness to God. So God chose the Gentiles to serve Him, since Israel would not. As H. H. Halley said,

> Paul is not discussing the predestination of individuals to salvation or condemnation, but is asserting God's absolute sovereignty in the choice and management of nations for world functions.[2]

Romans 9-11 is all about vocational election to service, not individual election to eternal life. And if you have believed the saving message, you are part of the remnant, too.

---

[2] H. H. Halley, *Bible Handbook*, 17th ed (Grand Rapids, MI: Zondervan, 1965), 527.

17

Chosen in Him
(Ephesians 1:4-5)

Christ is the principally elected one and God has chosen a corporate body to be included in him.
WILLIAM KLEIN[1]

1. Introduction

IF I EVER GET really sick, I plan on moving back to Canada.

The U.S.'s mix of socialist healthcare and crony capitalism makes medical costs practically unaffordable for most Americans. One of the quickest ways to go bankrupt in this country is to get sick. Thankfully, our family is covered by my wife's health insurance plan. The kids and I get our benefits through her. Whenever I sign up to see a new

---

[1] William Klein, *The New Chosen People: A Corporate View of Election* (Grand Rapids, MI: Zondervan, 1990), 180.

doctor, I have to identify my wife as the primary. I'm the secondary. She's the insurance holder. I'm just riding her coattails.

The way our family gets medical benefits through our union with my wife is analogous to the way we are elect through our union with Christ, which is the subject of Eph 1:4-5.

2. Chosen "In Him"

Paul says that God chose the Jews[2] "in Him." It's an interesting expression, one that should be familiar from our studies in the individual/corporate pattern of election in the OT.

When God elected a person for a specific task, that choice was often implicitly corporate. When God chose Aaron to be high priest, his descendants were chosen in him, too.

That's the same kind of positional truth that we see here about the meaning of being "in Christ." Although many interpreters assume that God predestines individuals directly, Paul presents God's election instrumentally, as being in and through Christ. That is entirely consistent with the OT evidence we looked at.

---

[2] As John McRay argues, the pronouns in Ephesians show that Paul is thinking in terms of "us" Jews, writing to "you" Gentiles, who eventually become "we" the one body of Christ. See John McRay, "Ephesians, Theology of," in Walter A. Elwell, *Evangelical Dictionary of Theology*. See http://www.biblestudytools.com/dictionaries/bakers-evangelical-dictionary/ephesians-theology-of.html. Accessed June 15, 2017.

In fact, Paul's argument refers to what is true *in Christ* or *in Him*, no fewer than eleven times in Ephesians 1 alone (*in Christ Jesus*, 1:1; *in Him*, 1:4, 7, 9, 10, 11, 13; *in Christ*, 1:3, 10, 12, 20). Here are some of the relevant verses in Ephesians 1-2[3]:

- "in Christ"...blessed us with every spiritual blessing (1:3)
- "in Him"...chosen before creation (1:4)
- "by Jesus Christ"...predestined to adoption (1:5)
- "in the Beloved"...made accepted (1:6)
- "in Him"...redeemed and forgiven (1:7)
- "in Himself"...God's purpose and will were manifested (1:9)
- "in Christ/in Him"...everything was gathered together (1:10)
- "in Him"...obtained an inheritance (1:11a)
- "in Him"...was predestined (1:11b)
- "in Christ"...the Christian has trusted (1:12)
- "in Christ"...heard and believed (1:13)
- "in Him"...are sealed with the Spirit (1:13)
- "with Christ"...made alive (2:5)
- "in Christ Jesus"...sits in heavenly places (2:6)

---

[3] I have adapted and expanded this from a list given by William G. MacDonald, "The Biblical Doctrine of Election," in *The Grace of God and the Will of Man*, ed. Clark H. Pinnock (Minneapolis, MN: Bethany House Publishers, 1989), 222.

- "in Christ Jesus"…God shows grace and kindness (2:7)
- "in Christ Jesus"…created for good works (2:10)

You cannot help but see that these blessings are all strongly Christocentric. You might think of predestination as something that happens directly to you, but for Paul, Christ is the One Who is foremost in God's mind in the act of election. He is the primary insurance beneficiary. You only benefit in and through Him.

3. The Positional Implication

Paul says that election happens *in Christ*, but how can you be "in" Him (Eph 1:4)?

The Greek word *en* usually indicated when some*thing* was literally *in* something else, such as a person's being *in* a house. It was not typically used to indicate one person being inside another person because that normally doesn't happen (pregnancy notwithstanding). And yet, that's what Paul meant here. We are in Christ!

Paul is stating a positional truth. Richard S. Beals and Earl Radmacher explain:

> When we follow Paul's use of the expression, we discover that to be *in Christ* means that in a real sense the Christian has been placed, located *within* Christ. *In*

> *Christ* signifies that whatever Jesus Christ
> is before God the Father, *the believer
> shares his identity*, because he or she is
> *within* the Savior. It is the Father giving
> the believer the exalted status that Christ
> in all His glory now holds. It is the Chris-
> tian's *full identification with Jesus Christ* in
> the eyes of the Father.[4]

That is exactly what we saw in our examina-
tion of the individual/corporate pattern in divine
election. Priests were chosen to serve as priests
because they were "in Aaron" and shared his identity.

Likewise, believers are predestined insofar as
they are "in Christ" and so share His identity. That
is how predestination relates to the *en Christo* (in
Christ). You are not individually elected from all
eternity. The group is. The Body of Christ is. And
you are put "in Christ" when you believe in Him.
As Beals and Radmacher go on:

> When I believed, at that point I was
> placed *in Christ*. I become in God's sight
> what Jesus is. At the time of the conscious
> act of faith, through becoming one with
> Christ, I was chosen *in Him*. I was not
> chosen to believe, but having believed
> I was chosen for *all that He is*. Is Christ

---

[4] R. S. Beals, Jr. and Earl D. Radmacher, *Ephesians: Life and Love in Christ*
(Chino Valley, AZ: One World Press, 2012), 6-7.

without sin in the reckoning of the Father? So am I (Eph 1:4, 7). Is Christ risen from the dead? In the reckoning of God, even now so am I (Eph 2:6), although the event waits the Lord's reappearing (1 Cor 15:51-52). Was Christ chosen before the foundation of the world? So am I, although my being chosen did not take place until the day that through faith I was placed "in him." As a believer I was chosen "before the foundation of the world," but only through being "in Him."[5]

Andy Johnson, commenting on this idea from Ephesians and explaining how it applies to election in 1 Thessalonians, concurred:

We will therefore assume that Jesus is indeed God's primary Elect One and that others are secondarily elect in him. Hence, individual Thessalonians are indeed elect and holy, but only insofar as they are "in Christ," God's Elect, Holy One; that is, only insofar as they are an ongoing part of a corporate body of the risen, cruciform Christ in Thessalonica.[6]

---

[5] Beals and Radmacher, *Ephesians*, 14-15.
[6] Andy Johnson, *1 & 2 Thessalonians* (Grand Rapids, MI: Eerdmans, 2016), 42.

4. "Holy and Blameless"

God has a purpose for electing His people. Paul says the Jews were chosen to be "holy and blameless."

Although some take this as a reference to forensic justification, Paul is simply restating the purpose of Israel's election, i.e., they had the vocation of being a holy people:

> "And you shall be holy to Me, for I the Lord am holy, and have separated you from the peoples, that you should be Mine" (Lev 20:26).

This is a call for ethical righteousness, not a statement of being predestined for Christ's imputed righteousness.

And as C. Gordon Olson explains, this vocation is now shared by all believers: "all believers are now appointed to an office in the body of Christ with the obligation to be 'holy and blameless before Him.'"[7]

All believers are supposed to develop ethical righteousness in their union with Christ. And, I believe, this purpose is related to rewards in the kingdom.

---

[7] C. Gordon Olson, *Beyond Calvinism and Arminianism: An Inductive Mediate Theology of Salvation,* Third Edition (Lynchburg, VA: Global Gospel Publishers), 336.

5. "To Adoption as Sons"

Paul says that God predetermined the Jews to be "adopted as sons" (Eph 1:5) and for obtaining "an inheritance" (Eph 1:11). Although, once again, these are taken as synonyms for receiving eternal life, in point of fact, they are rewards concepts that refer to ruling with Messiah in His kingdom.

When Paul says that God "predestined [or predetermined] us to adoption as sons," we know this "adoption" was a corporate and conditional blessing given to Israel. For example:

> For I could wish that I myself were accursed from Christ for *my brethren, my countrymen according to the flesh*, who are *Israelites, to whom pertain the adoption*, the glory, the covenants, the giving of the law, the service of God, and the promises; of whom are the fathers and from whom, according to the flesh, Christ came, who is over all, the eternally blessed God. Amen (Rom 9:3-5, emphasis added).

Elsewhere, Paul explained that Christ was born under the Mosaic Law so that He could redeem and adopt the Jews:

> But when the fullness of time had come, God sent forth His Son, born of a woman, born under the law, *to redeem those who were under the law*, that we might receive

the adoption of sons (Gal 4:4-5, emphasis added).

Paul says that God predestined "us" for an inheritance (Eph 1:11). There is a strong connection between "adoption" and "inheritance" insofar as the former was for obtaining the latter. In the Roman world, adoption was a necessary legal step to inherit the adoptive father's estate. It was a common way for two families to unite for economic and political gain. And more interesting still, adoption was one of the ways in which Roman emperors passed their authority to their successors.

The following quote is from Michael Peppard. I know it is a long quote, but it is excellent. I believe it sheds much light on what the NT means when it speaks of our sonship and adoption:

> When one investigates father-son relationships in the Roman family, one finds a strong emphasis on inheritance and transmission of power. Despite the appearance of smooth patrilineal transitions, Roman familial and political succession exhibited a tension between meritocratic and dynastic ideologies. However, the Romans had a technique at their disposal—the adoption of adult men—that enabled the different ideologies of succession to coexist for hundreds of

> years. To read a list of powerful Roman men is necessarily to read a list of *adopted* Roman men: Scipio Africanus the Younger, Caesar Augustus, Tiberius, Germanicus, Gaius Caligula, Nero, Pliny the Younger, Trajan, Hadrian, Antoninus Pius, Marcus Aurelius, Lucius Verus, and Constantius I, to name only the most famous....
>
> From these social realities, the scholar of early Christianity can carry the following conclusions into his or her work: In the Roman worldview, sonship did not primarily point *backward* to begetting, but *forward* to inheritance, often through the medium of adoption.[8]

When Paul spoke of our adoption and inheritance, he was invoking the familiar language and customs of the Roman Empire (and the OT) regarding passing on an inheritance to a child (not to mention how rulership was passed on to a successor).

Paul was saying that God decided beforehand to do the same to the Jews and Gentiles who

---

[8] Michael Peppard, "Powerful Sons Were Adopted Sons: A Roman Imperial Perspective." See http://www.bibleinterp.com/articles/pep368014.shtml. Accessed July 2, 2015. See also Michael Peppard, *The Son of God in the Roman World: Divine Sonship in its Social and Political Context* (New York, NY: Oxford University Press, 2012).

believed in Christ. They, too, would receive an inheritance.

As Jesus made plain in the Parable of the Minas, He is looking for believers to rule with Him in His kingdom (Luke 19:11-27). Paul said believers are meant to "reign with Him" (2 Tim 2:12), that is, with Jesus.

Paul spoke about the dual inheritance in Rom 8:17, of being "heirs of God" and of others being "co-heirs with Christ."

As Ephesians 1 makes clear, God is now offering the opportunity to rule to both Jew and Gentile, to whoever believes in Christ and endures in the faith. In Him, all believers can be adopted as sons[9] and have a special inheritance in the kingdom.

6. Conclusion

An individualistic interpretation of Eph 1:4-5 misses Paul's corporate and Christocentric emphases. Paul was making an argument about the blessings that God first gave the Jews and which He later offered to the Gentiles on an equal basis, i.e., in Christ. God reckons all the blessings given to Christ as belonging to the believer—whether Jew or Gentile—through faith in Him.

---

[9] There is a sense in which all believers are adopted as sons at the moment of faith (cf., John 1:12).

In other words, Eph 1:4-5 is not about God's individually predestining people to heaven or hell, but God's decision to have a new corporate entity, the Body of Christ, composed of Jews and Gentiles, who will be adopted by Him, given a special inheritance, and rewarded with ruling with Christ in the Messianic kingdom.

I thank God that my family gets the blessing of healthcare through union with my wife. But the blessings of being in union with Christ, of participating in His own election, are far, far, greater.

18

Chosen for Salvation
(2 Thessalonians 2:13)

*We fear things in proportion
to our ignorance of them.*
CHRISTIAN NESTELL BOVEE

1. Introduction

I HAVE A RECURRING nightmare in which I am still in high school and sign up for a science class I never attend. At the end of the semester I suddenly realize I have a year of classwork to do, or I won't graduate.

Given the fact that I graduated from high school over 20 years ago, that is an irrational fear!

The Thessalonians had an irrational fear, too. They worried they had missed the Rapture and were in the Tribulation. So Paul reminded them of a simple fact: they were "chosen for salvation" (2 Thess 2:13).

2. The Thessalonians Were "Chosen"

When Paul wrote that God "chose" the Thessalonians, he used the unusual word *heilato*.[1] Charles Ryrie notes that, "The word Paul uses to describe the choosing is an unusual one and is used nowhere else in the New Testament of divine election."[2] But it is used for God's choice of Israel in the OT. As Andy Johnson notes, "As is apparent from a comparison of Deut 7:6-7 with Deut 14:2, a form of this verb is interchangeable with the cognate verb of the noun "election", used in 1 Thess 1:4."[3] Likewise, Leon Morris explains it is used "in the LXX of the choosing of Israel in Deut 26:18."[4]

This is significant because, as we saw in earlier chapters, Israel's election was not an individual election to eternal life. Hence, Paul's word choice in 2 Thess 2:13 already points away from the traditional predestinarian interpretation. But let's not jump to conclusions before looking at the context.

---

[1] Samuel Fisk, *Election and Predestination: Keys to a Clearer Understanding* (Bicester, England: Penfold Book & Bible House, 1997), 138.

[2] Charles C. Ryrie, *First & Second Thessalonians* (Chicago, IL: Moody, 2001), 119.

[3] Andy Johnson, *1 & 2 Thessalonians* (Grand Rapids, MI: Eerdmans, 2016), 202.

[4] Leon Morris, *1 and 2 Thessalonians*, Revised Edition (Grand Rapids, MI: Eerdmans, 1984), 136; cf. Ryrie, *Thessalonians*, 119.

3. "From the Beginning"

Paul told the Thessalonians they were chosen for salvation "from the beginning."[5] When was that?

You may assume this is the timeless eternity of traditional predestination theology. However, the Greek for "from the beginning" is *archēs*. It is used in connection with the first moments of creation (Matt 24:21); the creation of Adam and Eve (Matt 19:4, 8); to describe someone's long standing evil character (John 8:44; 1 John 3:8); the beginning of a ministry (such as Jesus': Luke 1:2; John 15:27; 16:4); to remind readers of something they had been taught in the recent past (1 John 1:1; 2:24); and to describe how the Great Tribulation will be worse than anything seen since the beginning of the world (Matt 24:21; Mark 13:19). In other words, these uses of *archēs* all occur *in time*. They are all "beginnings" at some point *in history*—whether it's thousands of years in the past (e.g. the creation of Adam and Eve), or just a few months before (e.g., the beginning of a ministry). They do not refer to a point *beyond* time,

---

[5] Actually, there is a variant reading in the critical text of NA[28] that reads "firstfruits" (*aparchēn*). However, Andy Johnson takes this reading and still argues that election is for service: "God's rescue of this audience in the *missio Dei* was not only for the sake of their own salvific benefit but also for the purpose of enlisting them in that mission" (Johnson, *1 & 2 Thessalonians*, p. 202). Johnson takes election in the Thessalonians correspondence as "election to representation" whereby a corporate people, the elect community, "can represent *God to others* by reflecting the righteousness and holiness of God to the nonelect" (Ibid., p. 319).

such as the timeless eternity of predestinarian thought.

If "from the beginning" actually refers to a point in time, when did the Thessalonians become chosen for salvation? When they believed in Jesus for eternal life. As G. G. Findlay explained,

> "It is doubtful where *ap'archēs* (from the beginning) looks further back than to the time *when God's call in the gospel reached the Thessalonians*; without some indication in the context, the reader would hardly think here of a *pretemporal* election. The *eklogia* (election) of 1 Thess 1:4 was associated *with the arrival of the gospel at Thessalonica* (1 Thess 1:5, 9)."[6]

In other words, the Thessalonians were chosen *when they first believed the saving message*. But chosen for what?

4. "For Salvation"

Paul told the Thessalonians they were chosen *for salvation (sōtēria)*. What kind of salvation?

Predestinarian thought assumes this refers to eternal salvation. They often wrongly assume that *salvation* is a technical term for deliverance *from*

---

[6] Emphasis added. Quoted in Samuel Fisk, *Election and Predestination: Keys to a Clearer Understanding* (Bicester: Penfold Book and Bible House, 1997), 139.

hell when, in fact, most uses of the word *save* or *salvation* actually refer to earthly salvation.[7] As Bob Wilkin summarizes the evidence:

> And did you realize that in the New Testament only three in ten uses of *salvation* (*sōtēria*) and *save* (*sōzō*) refer to salvation from eternal condemnation and to obtaining eternal life? That means 70% of the time in the New Testament the words save or salvation do not mean what most people think they mean.[8]

For example, remember when Peter walked on water? He took a few steps, became afraid, started sinking, and cried out, "Lord, save me!" (Matt 14:28-30). What kind of salvation was Peter referring to? Clearly, he wasn't suddenly worried about *hell*—he wanted to be saved from *drowning*!

Wilkin gives many other examples of how *save* and *salvation* most often refer to deliverance from physical threats and dangers in this life—from war, disease, famine, sickness, enemies and so on.

Given the fact the Bible talks about several kinds of salvation, what kind is it here?

I believe Paul is talking about being saved from death in the Tribulation. I will give some contextual reasons why in just a moment.

---

[7] See Robert N. Wilkin, *The Ten Most Misunderstood Words in the Bible* (Denton, TX: Grace Evangelical Society, 2012), Chap. 3
[8] Ibid., 33-34.

While this is the only place in 2 Thessaslonians in which *sōtēria* appears, Paul also used it in 1 Thess 5:9. Understanding the meaning of *salvation* there will help us understand it in 2 Thess 2:13.

First, Paul taught them about the Rapture. The Thessalonians were worried that dead believers would miss the Lord's coming. Paul taught them that all Church age believers will see the Lord at His coming, even if they have to be resurrected first:

> *We* who are alive and remain until the coming of the Lord will by no means precede those who are asleep. For the Lord Himself will descend from heaven with a shout, with the voice of an archangel, and with the trumpet of God. *And the dead in Christ will rise first.* Then *we* who are alive and remain shall be caught up together with them in the clouds to meet the Lord in the air. And thus *we* shall always be with the Lord. Therefore comfort one another with these words (1 Thess 4:15a-18, emphasis added).

Note that when Paul spoke about this event he used "we." He spoke of himself and the Thessalonians—and by extension all Church-age believers. All believers who are alive when the Lord comes will be caught up to meet Him in the air. So will all believers who died beforehand, only, they will be resurrected first.

Second, Paul warned them about the destruction to come. When Paul described the terrible events of the Tribulation, or the Day of the Lord, he switched to the third person:

> While *they* are saying, "Peace and safety!" then destruction will come upon *them* suddenly like labor pains upon a woman with child, and *they* will not escape (1 Thess 5:3, emphasis added).

In other words, the destruction he described would happen to *other people*, to unbelievers, not to *believers*.

Finally, Paul switched back to "we" and "us" and assured the believers that since they were "sons of lights" and "sons of the day," God did not appoint them to experience the wrath and destruction of the Day of the Lord, but to obtain salvation:

> For God has not destined us *for wrath*, but *for obtaining salvation* through our Lord Jesus Christ, who died for us, so that whether we are awake or asleep, we will live together with Him (1 Thess 5:9, emphasis added).

What would the Thessalonians be saved from? Not from hell, but from God's wrath during the Tribulation. Kevin Zuber explains:

> If the "wrath" in 1:10 is the same "wrath" referred to here in 5:9, it would seem obvious that "wrath to come" will arrive not on some undefined "day of judgment" but on and with the day of the Lord.[9]

And how would they be saved from those events? They would be raptured before it started.[10]

That is also what *salvation* means in 2 Thess 2:13.

5. Chosen to Be Saved from Tribulation

What were the Thessalonians chosen to be saved from?

The context strongly suggests that hell is not in view. Rather, the Thessalonians feared they were in the Tribulation period, but Paul assured them those terrible events had not yet begun:

> Now, brethren, concerning the coming of our Lord Jesus Christ and our gathering together to Him, we ask you, not to be soon shaken in mind or troubled, either

---

[9] Kevin D. Zuber, "Paul and the Rapture: 1 Thessalonians 4–5," *Evidence for the Rapture: A Biblical Case for Pretribulationism*, ed. John Hart (Chicago, IL: Moody, 2015), 166.
[10] Ibid., 166-67.

by spirit or by word or by letter, as if from us, *as though the day of Christ had come* (2 Thess 2:1-2, emphasis added).

Nevertheless, the Thessalonians were not convinced. To still their fears, Paul instructed them about the signs that must happen before those terrible events:

Let no one deceive you by any means; for *that Day will not come* unless the falling away comes first, and the man of sin is revealed, the son of perdition, who opposes and exalts himself above all that is called God or that is worshiped, so that he sits as God in the temple of God, showing himself that he is God (2 Thess 2:3-4).

And for this reason God will send *them* strong delusion, that *they* should believe the lie, that *they* all may be condemned *who did not believe* the truth but had pleasure in unrighteousness (2 Thess 2:11-12, emphasis added).

Notice the emphasis on *who* would experience these things: *them, they, those who did not believe.* There were terrible events coming, but as we already saw in 1 Thessalonians, those horrors would be experienced *by other people.* It would happen to those *who didn't believe* in Christ but who believed "the lie" and "strong delusion" instead.

And what would happen to the Thessalonians? Would they suffer, too? No. As Paul assured them:

> But we are bound to give thanks to God always for you, brethren beloved by the Lord, because God from the beginning *chose you for salvation* through sanctification by the Spirit and belief in the truth, to which He called you by our gospel, for the obtaining of the glory of our Lord Jesus Christ (2 Thess 2:13-14, emphasis added).

They were chosen to be saved from the horrific future events that Paul just described, i.e., "the day of the Lord" (2 Thess 2:2); "the son of destruction" (2 Thess 2:3); "the mystery of lawlessness" (2 Thess 2:7); "the activity of Satan" (2 Thess 2:9); "the deception of wickedness" (2 Thess 2:10); and the "deluding influence" (2 Thess 2:11).

And how would they be saved from that terrible day? Once again, through the Rapture,[11] or "the departure" (2 Thess 2:3).[12] As Cornelius Stam explained,

---

[11] William MacDonald, *Believer's Bible Commentary*, ed. Art Farstad (Dallas, TX: Thomas Nelson, 1995), 2041.

[12] Tommy Ice, H. Wayne House, and Nathan Holsteen argue that *the departure* is a reference to the Rapture. See Ice, Thomas D., "The Rapture in 2 Thessalonians 2:3" (2009). Available online: http://digitalcommons. liberty.edu/cgi/viewcontent.cgi?article=1081&context=pretrib_arch. Accessed September 10, 2017. H. Wayne House, "Is the Rapture Found in 2 Thessalonians 2:3?" Available online: http://www.pre-trib.org/data/

It is after discussing God's wrath upon this unbelieving world during the Tribulation, that the Apostle expresses his joy that God has chosen to save believers from this holocaust, "through sanctification of the Spirit and belief of the truth.[13]

The word 'salvation' has a wide range of meaning in Scripture, and in the light of its context, 'salvation' here is from the Tribulation, not from the judgment of the Great White Throne.[14]

The moment the Thessalonians believed in Christ for eternal life they were *set apart from the world* (2 Thess 2:13; cf. Rom 15:16) and chosen to be saved from God's Tribulation wrath by being raptured.[15]

6. Conclusion

The Thessalonians were not concerned about individual predestination to eternal life or death. That issue is never raised in 1 or 2 Thessalonians.

---

pdf/House-ADefenseoftheRapture.pdf. Accessed September 10, 2017. Nathan D. Holsteen, "Paul and the Rapture: 2 Thessalonians," *Evidence for the Rapture*, 184-86.

[13] Cornelius Stam, *Commentary on the Epistles of Paul to the Thessalonians* (Chicago, IL: Berean Bible Society, 1984), 135.

[14] Ibid., 134.

[15] David Dunlap, *Limiting Omnipotence: The Consequences of Calvinism* (Port Colborne, ON: Gospel Folio Press, 2004), 94.

The context is all about the Rapture and the terrible Day of the Lord. Paul assured the Thessalonians they were "chosen for salvation." The moment they believed in Jesus for eternal life, they became members of the Body of Christ, and were chosen to be raptured away before the Tribulation began.

In sum, this passage isn't about individual election to eternal life or death, but about God's promise to save the Body of Christ from the wrath of the Tribulation.

19

Enduring All Things
(2 Timothy 2:10)

It behooves a father to be blameless
if he expects his child to be.
HOMER

1. Introduction

NOW THAT I HAVE children, I understand the strong hopes and dreams parents can have for them.

I want the very best for my kids. I want them to prosper in every way (3 John 2). I want them to have a better life than I had. I want them to have a life-changing relationship with God. I pray daily for God's love to take deep root in their hearts. And that is what I'm working to achieve in their lives, even though it isn't always easy.

Likewise, Paul wanted his spiritual children to experience the fullness of salvation that God intended for them, and he was prepared to work for it. Here is what Paul wrote:

> Therefore I endure all things for the sake of *the elect*, that they also may *obtain the salvation* which is in Christ Jesus with eternal glory. This is a faithful saying:
> For if we died with Him,
>   We shall also live with Him.
>   If we endure,
>   *We shall also reign with Him.*
>   If we deny Him,
>   He also will deny us.
>   If we are faithless,
>   He remains faithful;
>   He cannot deny Himself.
> Remind them of these things, charging them before the Lord not to strive about words to no profit, to the ruin of the hearers. Be diligent to *present yourself approved to God*, a worker who does not need to be ashamed, rightly dividing the word of truth (2 Tim 2:10-15 NKJV, emphasis added).

The traditional interpretation of this passage is that Paul endured all things so the individuals God had predestined from all eternity to have eternal life would get it.

I believe that interpretation is mistaken.

There are several terms that must be examined here to determine Paul's meaning.

2. The Elect

Who are "the elect"? There are at least two options.

The elect can be believers in Jesus Christ, members of the Body of Christ. You become elect the moment you believe in Jesus for everlasting life. At that point, you receive numerous benefits "in Him" (see Ephesians 1).

Or *the elect* may be qualitative, and refers to the kind of faithful believers who will receive special privileges in the Messianic kingdom. Think of what Jesus said in the Parable of the Wedding Feast about many being called, but few being chosen.

Either way, do not assume *the elect* refers to individuals predestined from all eternity to have eternal life.

3. Salvation

And what kind of "salvation" does Paul want the elect to obtain?

We know enough now not to assume this is salvation from hell.

And clearly, this salvation is not the initial moment of being born again since that is past, and the salvation Paul pictures is still future.

I believe the salvation experience Paul has in mind is ruling with Christ in the Messianic Kingdom. Consider what he says in the very next verses:

> This is a faithful saying:
> For if we died with Him,
> We shall also live with Him.
> If we endure,
> *We shall also reign with Him* (2 Tim 2:11-12a NKJV, emphasis added).

The salvation Paul wants for the elect is related to reigning with Christ. This is a reference to ruling with Christ in the Messianic kingdom. God created man to rule (Gen 1:26-28), and that purpose will find its ultimate fulfillment when Jesus is reigning in Jerusalem and faithful believers are rewarded with positions of authority within that kingdom (Luke 19:11-21). Only then will we fully realize the abundant life Christ offers the faithful (John 10:10).

Think of the Israelites. God saved them from Egyptian slavery. But that was not all that God wanted for them. He wanted the Israelites to experience abundant life in the Promised Land. Likewise, there is more to the salvation God wants for you than to be born again. He wants you to rule with Christ in the kingdom.

4. Denied or Approved

However, while all believers are saved in the sense of having everlasting life, not all believers will be saved in the sense of reaching their full potential of ruling with Christ in the kingdom. Not every Israelite that was saved from Egyptian bondage entered the Promised Land. Likewise, not every born-again believer will rule with Christ. Some will be denied the privilege.

> If we deny Him,
> He also will deny us (2 Tim 2:12b NKJV).

If you have not endured in the faith and have denied Jesus in this life, then He will deny you.

What will you be denied? What Paul just referred to—reigning with Him.

You'll be like the wicked servant in the Parable of the Minas, who gets his talent taken away and is denied the privilege of ruling over any cities in the kingdom (see Luke 19:11-21). Or you'll be like the guest at the wedding feast, who is kicked out of the party into the outer darkness, because he wasn't wearing the proper wedding garments (representing acts of personal righteousness, see Chap. 10).

Paul did not want that outcome for any believer. He wanted all believers to rule with Christ in the Messianic kingdom. He wanted them to be co-heirs and to be co-glorified with Christ. That's why he endured all things for their sake.

5. Conclusion

In 2 Tim 2:10, Paul was not teaching about individual election to eternal life or death. Instead, he was urging Timothy to be a good pastor, one that would do everything in his power to help God's people become the kind of overcomers who will reign with Christ in the kingdom. There was no guarantee that would happen. They could be denied rulership.

I don't know what the future will hold for my three kids, but my desire is to see all of them prosperous, and I will do all that I can to make sure they are. That's how Paul felt about the Christians in his day. That's how Paul would feel about you. How will you measure up? Will you be approved or disapproved? Will you reign with Jesus or be denied?

20

Elect According to Foreknowledge
(1 Peter 1:2)

*Short summary of every Jewish holiday: They tried
to kill us, we won, let's eat.*
JOKE

1. Introduction

I AM ALWAYS AMAZED when I read about the
history of the Jewish people and how many world-
ly powers have tried to wipe them out.

The bodies of the Pharaohs have turned to
dust in their crumbling pyramids, but the Jewish
people live on.

The Roman emperors have little more to show
for their efforts than a few columns for tourists to
photograph, but the Jewish people live on.

The Tsars were killed, and the Communists
fell, but the Jewish people live on.

The Fuhrer and his thousand year Reich lasted little more than a decade, but the Jewish people live on.

The Jews have been maligned, beaten, persecuted, jailed, and killed, but never wiped out. There were times when it seemed like they were on the brink of destruction, but God was not done with them. The Jewish people live on.

They lived on in Peter's day, too.

2. Elect According to Foreknowledge

> To the pilgrims of the Dispersion in Pontus, Galatia, Cappadocia, Asia, and Bithynia, *elect according to the foreknowledge of God the Father*, in sanctification of the Spirit, for obedience and sprinkling of the blood of Jesus Christ (1 Pet 1:1-2a, NKJV, emphasis added).

The reason why Peter called his readers "elect" is because he was writing to Jewish believers. The word "elect" modifies "pilgrims of the Dispersion" (*diaspora*), which is a term for Jews living in Gentile countries.[1]

Additionally, Gary Derickson suggests they were not only elect as Jews, but also elect in the

---

[1] Gary Derickson, "The First Epistle of Peter," in *The Grace New Testament Commentary* (Denton, TX: Grace Evangelical Society, 2010), 2:1145.

sense of being chosen to be pilgrims: "The readers were chosen to be pilgrims and hence to share in Christ's sufferings."[2]

Either way, they are not elect as individuals to have eternal life.

3. According to Foreknowledge

What did Peter mean by saying his readers were elect "according to the foreknowledge of God"?

I think he was simply reinforcing that the Jews were God's chosen people. For example, Paul used the same language:

> God has not rejected His people whom He foreknew (Rom 11:2a, emphasis added).

God knew the Jews beforehand, back when He first called Abraham out of Ur.

This is not foreknowledge in the sense of a choice made in a timeless eternity, but simply means the Jews were the chosen people from the beginning.

And Paul was right—God had "not cast away His people." In fact, Peter's readers were evidence of that. They were a remnant of Jews who believed in Christ for eternal life.

And they were called to fulfill Israel's calling, that is, to obey God and to become a holy people,

---

[2] Ibid.

for "sanctification of the Spirit, for obedience and sprinkling of the blood of Jesus Christ" (1 Pet 1:2).

4. Conclusion

There's no good reason to think this verse finally proves that God has chosen certain individuals to everlasting life. Peter here affirmed what the whole Bible affirms, that the Jews are God's chosen people. That does not mean God has not also chosen other people for other purposes. As we've seen again and again, election is often for service, and that service is usually to bring blessings to the world. The fact that these Jewish believers were in the Diaspora only gave them more opportunity to be used to bless those around them.

21

Make Your Calling and Election Sure (2 Peter 1:10-11)

When it comes to life the critical thing is whether
you take things for granted
or take them with gratitude.
G. K. CHESTERTON

1. Introduction

HOLLY HOLM, "THE PREACHER'S DAUGHTER,"
was already a multiple-time world champion in
boxing before signing a contract with Ultimate
Fighting Championships.

You would think she had nothing left to prove,
having defended her titles eighteen times in three
weight classes. But the UFC opened a whole new
professional horizon. Holm couldn't rest on her
laurels. It was her past accomplishments that
made any future accomplishments in the UFC

possible. Holm knew she would have to work harder than ever to make good on her new opportunities in the mixed martial arts world. After signing with UFC, Holm said, "Now their hard work is done and my hard work begins."[1]

That hard work paid off on November 14, 2015, when Holm faced the indomitable Ronda Rousey for the Bantamweight belt. "There is no way that she will beat Ronda Rousey," said the critical consensus. "Holly Holm has zero ground game. Do you see where I'm going with this? Once Rousey gets her on the ground it is all over."[2]

And yet, with a devastating kick to the head, Holm knocked Rousey out in the second round, and became the Bantamweight champion.

As many commentators later noted, "Hard work pays off."

I believe hard work pays off in the Christian life. You are called to serve, to be holy, and to do good. And God will reward you for that service, whether for good or for ill.

Second Peter 1:10-11 should be understood in light of the responsibility we have as those called by God. It is not about individual predestination to eternal life or death, but a reminder to stay vigilant in your service to God.

---

[1] http://www.abqjournal.com/427336/sports/holly-holm-signs-contract-to-join-ufc.html
[2] http://cagepages.com/2014/07/11/holly-holm-will-beat-ronda-rousey/ Accessed January 5, 2016.

2. Called to What?

> Therefore, brethren, be even more diligent
> to make your call and election sure, for if
> you do these things you will never stum-
> ble (2 Pet 1:10).

The question is, what were they called to?

At the beginning of 2 Peter 1, the Apostle
wrote about the blessings that made living a holy
life possible. Believers are given "all things that
pertain to life and godliness" (2 Pet 1:3). It is
possible to even become partakers of the divine
nature (2 Pet 1:4).

However, while it is *possible* to grow in holiness,
that outcome is not *inevitable*. It is up to believers
to move beyond an initial faith in Christ to virtue,
knowledge, self-control, perseverance, godliness,
brotherly kindness, and love (2 Pet 1:4-7).

It should be apparent to all that 2 Peter 1 is
deeply concerned with spiritual growth. We have
good reason to conclude that Peter was not asking his readers to determine whether or not they
really believed since he assumed they did ("add
to your faith," 2 Pet 1:5). Nor was he calling their
eternal salvation into question.

Instead, they were called to holiness. They
were called to grow. They were called to clothe
themselves in acts of personal righteousness.

3. Elected to What?

If Peter's readers were called to holiness, what were they elected to?

Second Peter 1:11 provides the answer:

> Therefore, brethren, be even more diligent to make your call and election sure, for if you do these things you will never stumble; *for so an entrance will be supplied to you abundantly into the everlasting kingdom of our Lord and Savior Jesus Christ* (2 Pet 1:10-11, emphasis added).

Remember that Jesus told us to lay up treasure in heaven (Matt 6:20), and Paul compared doing good works to building with gold, silver and precious stones, but not everyone builds well (1 Cor 3:12). Peter was repeating that theme, picturing the time when all those treasures will finally be received by the overcomers who will receive an abundant entrance in the kingdom.

In his commentary on 2 Peter, Zane Hodges concurred with this interpretation:

> Here is one of the many verbal allusions in the Petrine epistles to the teaching Peter had heard from the Lord Jesus Christ Himself: "many are called, but few are chosen [*eklektoi*]" (Matt 20:16; 22:14).
>
> All Christians have been given *a royal summons* by God Himself, inviting them

to the glorious privilege of co-reigning with Christ in the life to come (2 Tim 2:12; Rev 2:26-27; 3:21). But not all Christians will be *chosen* to co-reign (cf. Rom 8:17b; 2 Tim 2:12).

Peter, therefore, wishes his readership to produce in their lifestyle appropriate verification that they are royal people, destined for high honor in the coming kingdom of God.[3]

We know that the only basis for *admission* to the kingdom is faith in Jesus for eternal life.[4] We also know there is a difference between *entering* the kingdom and *inheriting* it. Just as the OT provided for different levels of inheritance between descendants, so too the NT teaches that there will be degrees of reward given to believers at the Judgment Seat of Christ.

That's what is at issue in 2 Pet 1:10-11. Peter wanted his believing readers to have a rich kingdom entrance.

---

[3] Zane C. Hodges, "The Second Epistle of Peter" in *The Grace New Testament Commentary* (Denton, TX: Grace Evangelical Society, 2010), 2:1174.

[4] William MacDonald, *Believer's Bible Commentary*, ed. Art Farstad (Dallas, TX: Thomas Nelson, 1995), 2291.

4. Conclusion

When the Apostle Peter wrote about election, it was with Jewish believers in mind, but the general principles apply to all believers.

Peter urged believers to live a life worthy of reward, worthy of an abundant entrance in the Messianic kingdom. Those rewards will be given to believers who fulfill the calling to holiness and fulfill their vocational election to do good works (Eph 2:10), always with the ultimate goal of ruling with Christ (2 Tim 2:12) and becoming a joint-heir with Him (Rom 8:17).

Our future role in the kingdom is not guaranteed, but conditional. It depends on our diligence, obedience, and perseverance.

Rather than take it for granted, we should strive to confirm our calling to holiness and to make our election sure.

Holly Holm was crowned after a tremendous amount of hard work aimed at winning the prize. Should you pursue an abundant entrance in Christ's kingdom with any less dedication?

Conclusion

"So what did you conclude?" Bob asked. "Do you still believe the Bible teaches that God elects individuals to eternal life?"

"No. I haven't answered every question to my satisfaction," I answered, "but one thing is sure."

"What's that?"

"People will probably quibble here and there about my interpretation of this or that passage," I said, "but no one can come to Scripture, look at the evidence, and deny that 80-90% of the Biblical material shows that election is of people, places, and things *to service and reward, not to eternal life.*"

"I agree," Bob answered. "But that's not what's usually taught, is it?"

"No it isn't," I said. "Why is that? Why is it that we only ever hear about election to eternal life when the Bible is so clear about election to service?"

"It's because they've pre-decided," Bob said.

"Pre-decided in what sense?"

"They pre-decided what belongs to the doctrine of election and what doesn't. It's not that theologians don't see that when God chooses Aaron or when Jesus chooses the apostles that it's to service. It's that preachers and theologians have pre-decided that's not part of the *real* doctrine of election to begin with," Bob explained.

"So they've already filtered out most of the evidence without realizing it?"

"Exactly," Bob answered. "I'll always remember studying soteriology with Craig Glickman at Dallas Seminary. He made the point that a Biblical doctrine of soteriology is not only about those verses dealing with *regeneration*. Regeneration can be a sub-section in soteriology, but soteriology is bigger than that. It's about *all* the verses dealing with salvation and deliverance. And that's what you've done here with election. You tried dealing with all the verses, not just a handful of them."

"Well, I'll say this—I wish I had paid more attention to what the Bible actually says about election when I was younger. It would have saved me a lot of grief."

"Me, too," Bob said. "I'm sure this book will be of great 'service' to many believers."

Appendix

The Decrees of God

The earth with its store of wonders untold,
Almighty! thy power hath founded of old;
Hath 'stablished it fast by a changeless decree,
And round it hath cast like a mantle the sea.
ROBERT GRANT

1. Introduction

WHEN THEOLOGIANS WRITE OR talk about *the decrees of God*, it is usually in hushed and reverential tones.

These decrees are said to lay at the very heart of the mystery of predestination and election to eternal life. In fact, some theologians use "decree" as a blanket term to describe anything that God has willed about salvation.[1]

---

[1] For example, John M. Frame, *Systematic Theology: An Introduction to Christian Belief* (Phillipsburg, PA: P&R Publishing, 2013), 206-30.

There is a great and venerable tradition about God's decrees. But as a committed and unapologetic Biblicist, I have to measure those traditions by the Scriptures. And what do we find? They come up short. Very short!

The surprising truth is that, despite the emphasis that systematic theologians put on God's decrees in election, the Bible itself rarely mentions God's decrees. And the dozen or so verses that deal with them *never* concern an individual's eternal destiny.[2]

2. The Decrees of Men

By far the most common references to decrees in the Bible are to those of men, such as the legal decrees issued by kings and rulers.[3] Many of these legal decrees were considered unalterable (especially in the context of Median and Persian law[4]) as we see in Ezra 6:11, Esth 8:8, and Dan 6:8.

Ezra records numerous decrees made by different kings such as Artaxerxes, Darius, and

---

[2] It is interesting to read Sam Storms's Appendix on "The Divine Decrees," because he doesn't actually quote any Scripture that says God makes decrees about salvation. At the beginning of the Appendix he refers to some verses dealing with election, but spends the next six pages detailing the order of the divine decrees without examining the Scriptures that actually mention God's decrees. See Sam Storms, *Chosen for Life: The Case for Divine Election* (Wheaton, IL: Crossway, 2007), 213-19.
[3] Laurence M. Vance, *The Other Side of Calvinism*, Revised Edition (Pensacola, FL: Vance Publications, 1991, 1999), 255.
[4] J. Kenneth Grider, *A Wesleyan-Holiness Theology* (Kansas City, MO: Beacon Hill Press, 1994), 253.

Cyrus, e.g., such as whether Jerusalem and the Temple should be rebuilt or not (Ezra 4:19, 21).

Nebuchanezzar initially decreed that everyone should worship a golden image (Dan 3:10), only to relent and decree that no one should insult the God of Israel (Dan 3:29). He also decreed that the wise men of Babylon should interpret a dream for him (Dan 4:6).

Likewise, Darius decreed that all should tremble before the God of Daniel (Dan 6:23).

These are all practical, legal decrees, by governments over their subjects.

It is the same in the NT.

Caesar Augustus passed a decree that everyone in the Empire should be registered (Luke 2:1). And the first Christians confessed that Jesus was king, against Caesar's decree (Acts 17:7).

I'm sure you get the picture.

Decrees had to do with civil government and legally binding orders dealing with political matters and behavior.

Are God's decrees any different?

Although *theologians* often speak about God's eternal decrees, *the Bible* rarely mentions them. In the rare case in which God does decree something, it is never in connection with choosing individuals for eternal life or death, but always related to His governance of the world.

3. God's Decrees about Israel

There are several verses that mention God's decrees with respect to His rulings[5] or moral government of His people and the world. For example, there are two references to God's decreeing a covenant with Israel:

> Then Moses cried out to the Lord, and the Lord showed him a piece of wood. He threw it into the water, and the water became sweet. There *the Lord made a decree and a law* for them, and there he tested them (Exod 15:25 NIV 1984, emphasis added).

The Lord went on to challenge the Israelites to obey Him so they would not be punished with disease as the Egyptians were. The decree was obviously not a pre-temporal choice of individuals for eternal life, but a part of the blessings and curses that were stipulated in God's covenant with Israel.

We find another reference to God's covenantal decree in Chronicles:

> He remembers his covenant forever,
> the promise he made, for a thousand generations,
> the covenant he made with Abraham,

---

[5] Ibid., 254.

the oath he swore to Isaac.
He confirmed it to Jacob *as a decree*,
to Israel as an everlasting covenant:
"To you I will give the land of Canaan
as the portion you will inherit" (1 Chron
16:15-17 NIV, emphasis added).

God promised to give Abraham the land of
Canaan. Although God's action in and through
Israel had a redemptive purpose, this was clearly
not an eternal selection of only some individuals
to eternal life.

4. God's Decrees about Moral Government

There are several mentions of decrees that
relate to God's moral governance (i.e., His moral
decrees) for the world:

Although they know *God's righteous decree* that those who do such things deserve
death, they not only continue to do these
very things but also approve of those who
practice them (Rom 1:32 NIV, emphasis
added).

Paul was saying if you break God's moral law,
you deserve to die.

Indeed, God's moral government is such that
He usually decrees that lawbreakers suffer disaster. For example, in Jeremiah we read,

> When the commander of the guard found
> Jeremiah, he said to him, "The Lord your
> God *decreed this disaster* for this place.
> And now the Lord has brought it about;
> he has done just as he said he would. All
> this happened because you people sinned
> against the Lord and did not obey him"
> (Jer 40:2-3 NIV, emphasis added).

Likewise, because of her sins, God decreed that Israel would suffer the catastrophe of the exile, in which only a remnant would return to the Holy Land:

> Though your people be like the sand by
> the sea, Israel, only a remnant will return.
> *Destruction has been decreed*, overwhelm-
> ing and righteous (Isa 10:22 NIV, empha-
> sis added).

During the exile, God also made a decree against King Nebuchadnezzar in a dream interpreted by Daniel:

> "This is the interpretation, Your Majesty,
> and this is *the decree* the Most High has
> issued against my lord the king" (Dan 4:24
> NIV, emphasis added).

And as part of that disaster judgment, God could decree to send deceiving spirits:

"So now the Lord has put a deceiving
spirit in the mouths of all these prophets
of yours. The Lord has *decreed disaster* for
you" (1 Kgs 22:23 NIV, emphasis added;
cf. 2 Chron 18:22).

All of these examples of God's moral governance of men are limited to temporal judgment,
not to eternal death. They are also, most often,
corporate decrees, dealing with peoples and
groups. What they do not deal with is an eternal
choice of some individuals to heaven and others
to hell.

5. God's Decrees about Creation

God's moral government over men is comple-
mented by His natural government of creation.
God has moral laws for moral creatures and
natural laws for nature. These natural laws are also
called His decrees.

For example, God "made a decree for the rain
and a path for the thunderstorm" (Job 28:26 NIV),
and God put the sea in its "decreed place, and
set bars and doors" for its boundaries (Job 38:10
KJV). He did the same for the sand:

"Do you not fear Me?" declares the LORD.
"Do you not tremble in My presence?
For I have placed the sand as a boundary
for the sea, *an eternal decree*, so it cannot

cross over it. Though the waves toss, yet they cannot prevail; Though they roar, yet they cannot cross over it" (Jer 5:22, emphasis added).

God has decreed that all the heavens—from the sun and moon to the angels—should praise His name. He has decreed they are to be established forever and "never pass away" (Ps 148:6).

6. Decrees about David and Jesus

God's decrees also encompass the vocational election of certain individuals, particularly David and Jesus. For example,

> I will surely tell of the decree of the Lord:
> He said to Me, "You are My Son,
> Today I have begotten You" (Ps 2:7).

This passage refers to God's enthronement of the king of Israel, who is regarded as His son. The NT applies this passage to Jesus. It is not a Trinitarian statement of His deity,[6] but, according to Paul, a reference to the Messiah's resurrection from the dead:

---

[6] Arno C. Gaebelein, *Gaebelein's Concise Commentary on the Whole Bible* (Neptune, NJ: Loizeaux Brothers, 1989), 457.

"We tell you the good news: What God
promised our ancestors he has fulfilled for
us, their children, by raising up Jesus. As it
is written in the second Psalm:
'You are my son; today I have become
your father.'
    God raised him from the dead so that he
will never be subject to decay. As God has
said,
'I will give you the holy and sure blessings
promised to David.'
    So it is also stated elsewhere:
'You will not let your holy one see decay.'
    "Now when David had served God's
purpose in his own generation, he fell
asleep; he was buried with his ancestors
and his body decayed. But the one whom
God raised from the dead did not see decay" (Acts 13:33-37 NIV).

This decree is vocational. It refers to the Messiah being begotten in the sense of being raised
from the dead, which vindicated His Messianic
claims, including being the true King of Israel.

7. Conclusion

I am amazed at the emphasis some systematic
theologians put on God's decrees regarding
His choosing of some people to eternal life

and others to eternal death. The entire debate between certain Calvinists (e.g., supralapsarians and infralapsarians) has to do with God's (non-existent) eternal decrees about salvation.

Perhaps the Westminster Confession of Faith best exemplifies this unbiblical emphasis on God's decrees in eternal election:

> III. By the decree of God, for the manifestation of his glory, some men and angels are predestinated unto everlasting life, and others foreordained to everlasting death.[7]

As we've seen, this is deeply mistaken. Strictly speaking, none of God's decrees are eternal (in the sense of being depicted as made in timeless eternity), and certainly none have to do with choosing which individuals have everlasting life and which will have everlasting death.

As Laurence Vance summarized the evidence,

> There is no such thing as God's eternal decree of predestination—except in the philosophical speculations and theological implications of Calvinism.[8]

If you've been worrying about God's decrees concerning your eternal destiny, you are thinking in unbiblical terms.

---

[7] Westminster Confession of Faith. See http://www.creeds.net/Westminster/c03.htm. Accessed June 20, 2017.
[8] Vance, *The Other Side*, 256.

Predestination

This is one of the two great labyrinths into which human minds are drawn: the question of free will versus predestination.
NEAL STEPHENSON

1. Introduction

I CUT MY THEOLOGICAL teeth on the doctrine of predestination. I was first introduced to it by some Calvinist friends. What they believed about predestination can be summed up in this quote by Charles Spurgeon:

> We shall never be able to escape from the doctrine of divine predestination—the doctrine that God has foreordained certain people unto eternal life.[1]

---

[1] C. H. Spurgeon, *Spurgeon at His Best: Over 2200 Striking Quotations*

There may be no other Biblical word that has so much theological baggage. The fog of tradition is *very* thick here. We've all experienced it. We've all lived in it. But if we can read the Bible while putting our traditions aside, just for a moment, there's hope of cutting through the fog.

Once again, the evidence may surprise you. Contra Spurgeon, *the Bible does not teach a predestination to heaven or hell.*[2]

There are six uses of the word for "to predestinate" (*proorizō*). We already discussed Rom 8:29-30 in chapter 13 and Eph 1:5, 11 in chapter 17. That leaves us with two verses: Acts 4:28 and 1 Cor 2:7. As we shall see, in neither case does God predestine anyone to eternal life (or death).

2. Predetermined to Take Place (Acts 4:27-28)

Peter and John had gone to the Temple to pray. They saw a forty-year old lame man and healed him in Jesus' name. This caught the attention of the other Temple-goers, so Peter and John began to preach that Jesus was raised from the dead and called on the people to repent of having put the Messiah to death. As a result, they were arrested by the priests and captain of the Temple guard. The next day, Peter and John were brought

---

from the World's Most Exhaustive and Widely-Read Sermon Series, ed. Tom Carter (Grand Rapids, MI: Baker, 1988), 164.

[2] J. Kenneth Grider, *A Wesleyan-Holiness Theology* (Kansas City, MO: Beacon Hill Press, 1994), 329.

forward by the high priests and scribes to give an account of what they were doing. They were warned not to preach in the name of Jesus. Peter and John refused, saying it was better to obey God than men. When Peter and John were released, they went to the other believers, they praised God, and someone cited Psalm 2 as evidence that the Jews would reject the Lord. And now we come to the verse in question:

> For truly in this city there were gathered together against your holy servant Jesus, whom you anointed, both Herod and Pontius Pilate, along with the Gentiles and the peoples of Israel, to do whatever your hand and your plan *had predestined to take place* (Acts 4:27-28 ESV, emphasis added).

Instead of *predestined,* the NKJV translates *proorizō* as *determined before.* I think that's the better reading. It helps us read the verse without the theological baggage that the word *predestination* has gathered over the centuries. The predetermining here is not about choosing individuals for eternal life or death, but about God's plans for the cross.

God determined beforehand that the Messiah would be rejected and killed.

God also determined beforehand to use
Herod, Pontius Pilate, and the people of Israel to
accomplish that purpose.

This is not a choice of individuals to eternal
life or death, but to service! It is a vocational pre-
determination.

3. Before the Ages (1 Corinthians 2:7)

The second verse about predestination is
found in 1 Cor 2:7-8, which says this:

> But we speak God's wisdom in a mystery,
> the hidden wisdom which God *predes-*
> *tined* before the ages to our glory; the
> wisdom which none of the rulers of this
> age has understood; for if they had under-
> stood it they would not have crucified the
> Lord of glory (emphasis added).

What is being predestined here?

There is no mention here of individuals being
predestined to eternal life.

Rather, this verse concerns God's predetermi-
nation that the Messiah would die for mankind. It
was a predestination to service.

4. Conclusion

Predestination can be an intimidating
topic, but it shouldn't be. The passages about

predestination in the NT are not hard to understand, and they are not what systematic theologians have made them out to be.

Although theological tradition will hammer home that predestination has to do with God's choosing individuals for everlasting life or death, the truth is, the Bible does not reflect that at all. As J. Kenneth Grider discovered,

> One of the most interesting theological finds I have made in recent years is that God's predestinating of us does not seem to have to do with eternal destiny.[3]

Grider is correct. Predestination does not have to do with individual eternal destiny. So far as we have seen, nowhere does the Bible teach such a doctrine.

However, it does concern God's determining to send His Son to be rejected by men, to die on the cross as an atonement for our sin, to rise from the dead, making salvation possible for all who believe in Him for eternal life (John 3:16). In other words, like the Biblical doctrine of election itself, predestination is to service, not eternal life.

---

[3] J. Kenneth Grider, "Predestination as Temporal Only." See http://www.libraryoftheology.com/writings/predestination/Predestination_As_Temporal_Only-KenGrider.pdf . See also Grider, *Wesleyan*, 249-55. .

Premillennialism and Acts 1:6

*The best way to find out if you can trust somebody
is to trust them.*
ERNEST HEMINGWAY

1. Introduction

AS WE HAVE STUDIED the Biblical doctrine of
election, we saw that many of the verses traditionally used to teach that God chooses individuals
for eternal life or death actually teach that God
chooses people for service, and if they are faithful,
they will be rewarded and will rule with Christ in
the Millennial kingdom.

The problem is, not everyone believes there
will be such a kingdom.

Certainly, since Augustine, the institutional
churches have rejected the idea that Jesus will
reign from Jerusalem in a literal kingdom on

earth. And readers who have inherited that Augustinian perspective will wonder—where does the Bible teach such a kingdom?

I trust that I have already pointed to some of the evidence for it, such as the Parable of the Talents (Luke 19:12-27), the Parable of the Wedding Feast (Matt 22:1-14, see chapter 10), as well as Paul's admonition to Timothy, that if believers endured they will "reign with Him" (2 Tim 2:12).

Many books have been written about the coming Millennial kingdom.[1] I won't repeat their efforts here.

Instead, by way of a short proof, I want to point you to the very last question the apostles asked Jesus.

2. Parting Words

> "Lord, is it at this time You are restoring the kingdom to Israel?" (Acts 1:6b).

No doubt this question had been on their minds from the very beginning, ever since they first heard Jesus announce the kingdom was "at hand," the great theme of His ministry (Mark 1:15). As believing Jews, the apostles longed for Israel's kingdom. They believed the Messiah would establish it when He came. So when Jesus arrived

[1] Start with Alva J. McClain, *The Greatness of the Kingdom: An Inductive Study of the Kingdom of God* (Winona Lake, IN: BMH Books, 2012).

on the scene, preaching the kingdom, their hopes were ignited.

Then disaster struck.

Jesus was arrested and executed by the Romans like a common criminal, and the apostles scattered.

Then, when Jesus was resurrected three days later, all the old hopes were re-ignited and burned even brighter.

"Will You do it soon?" they asked. "Will the kingdom be established *now*? Will Israel finally receive her promises?"

To the apostles, that question was absolutely vital.

But for most Christians today, it's absolutely bizarre.

Most Christians today would never think to ask it. Why not? They don't believe Israel will get a kingdom. They don't think anyone will. They reject the idea that God will give an earthly, still future, kingdom to anyone.

Instead, what most Christians believe is that Jesus preached a spiritual kingdom instead of an earthly one.

Is that true?

Whenever I am asked to defend my belief in a literal Messianic kingdom, I always turn to that pivotal question in Acts 1:6, "Lord, are You restoring the kingdom to Israel at this time?"

3. An Intensive Course

To understand the importance of the apostles' last question, remember that after Jesus rose from the dead, He not only spent forty days showing Himself alive to His disciples, He also spent that time teaching them about a very particular subject:

> To these He also presented Himself alive after His suffering, by many convincing proofs, appearing to them over a period of *forty days* and *speaking of the things concerning the kingdom of God* (Acts 1:3, emphasis added).

Jesus spent over a month teaching the apostles *about the kingdom of God.*

Of course, Jesus proclaimed the "gospel [good news] of the kingdom" from the very beginning of His ministry (cf. Mark 1:14). The message they were hearing was not entirely new. But when Jesus continued to teach about the kingdom during the forty days after His resurrection, there was a crucial difference—*the apostles were supernaturally enabled to understand what Jesus taught.*

Normally, the apostles were not the most gifted students. They were often confused about what Jesus meant. We often read about how they "did not understand these things at first" or "they did not understand this saying, and were afraid to ask Him" about it (John 12:16;

Mark 9:32; cf. Luke 2:50; 9:45; 18:34; John 16:19).

Their lack of understanding was a recurring problem during Jesus' pre-cross ministry.

But after Jesus' resurrection, the situation changed dramatically.

Luke supplies us with a crucial detail in connection with our Lord's forty days of kingdom teaching that explains why the apostles no longer had that problem.

> Now He said to them, "These are My words which I spoke to you while I was still with you, that all things which are written about Me in the Law of Moses and the Prophets and the Psalms must be fulfilled." *Then He opened their minds to understand the Scriptures* (Luke 24:44-45, emphasis added).

See that? Their minds were *opened*.

They supernaturally understood what Jesus was teaching.

In other words, Jesus was no longer addressing a befuddled band of followers. This is absolutely crucial to keep in mind when considering the last question they asked Him.

4. What the Question Implies

Think about the apostles' question for a moment and what it implies about their expectations and beliefs about the kingdom.

First, it implies the apostles expected *a literal kingdom*. Nothing in Jesus' teaching over the last forty days changed that basic expectation.

Second, it implies the apostles expected the kingdom to be *given to Israel*. During those forty days, Jesus evidently did not teach them that a new corporate entity, such as the Body of Christ, had replaced Israel or inherited her promises. The apostles still believed God had a plan for Israel and saw themselves as part of that plan.

Third, it implies the apostles knew the kingdom was *still future*. They knew they were not in the kingdom yet. They were not experiencing it then and there. They expected a still future fulfillment of the kingdom promises, though they hoped it was to begin within the hour.

Fourth, the question implies they expected the kingdom to be *pre-millennial*. They did not think the kingdom was already inaugurated in heaven (i.e., Amillenialism). Nor did they believe Jesus would come *after* the kingdom had already started (i.e., Postmillennialism). Rather, the apostles believed Jesus would be there at the beginning, *before it starts* (hence, "pre-"), in order to establish the kingdom personally.

5. Were the Apostles Being Carnal?

It is amazing to me how many Biblical commentators absolutely ridicule the apostles for asking this question. They ridicule them because they know their question implied Premillennialism (if not Dispensationalism), and they reject that theology.

So they say the apostles were being carnal.

They think the apostles still misunderstood Jesus.

Commentators say the apostles were clinging to old ideas about Israel's future, which they didn't realize Jesus repudiated.

Some commentators are more diplomatic about the apostles' failings than others.

For example, I. Howard Marshall very gently suggests the apostles were representative of Luke's readers "who had not yet realized that Jesus had transformed the Jewish hope of the kingdom of God by purging it of its nationalistic elements."[2] Silly apostles.

Likewise, F. F. Bruce wrote, "The question in v 6 appears to have been the last flicker of their former burning expectation of an imminent political theocracy with themselves as its chief executives."[3] In other words, the apostles were wrong to expect to rule with Christ in a literal

---

[2] I. Howard Marshall, *Acts* (Grand Rapids, MI: Eerdmans, 1996), 60.
[3] F. F. Bruce, *Commentary on the Book of the Acts* (Grand Rapids, MI: Eerdmans, 1981), 38.

kingdom, but they would know better soon enough (even though that's exactly what Jesus promised them, cf., Matt 19:28).

But few commentators are as refreshingly blunt as John Calvin:

> ...marvelous is their rudeness...they had been diligently instructed by the space of three whole years, they betray no less ignorance than if they had heard never a word. *There are as many errors in this question as words...*[T]hey declared thereby how bad scholars they were under so good a Master.[4]

As many errors in the question as words! That's a serious charge!

I appreciate Calvin's honesty. Calvin understood exactly what kind of kingdom theology is implied by the apostles' question, and he thought they were wrong, wrong, wrong.

Many commentators would agree with Calvin.

But is it really likely the apostles would be so wrong?

---

[4] John Calvin, "Commentary Upon the Acts of the Apostles, Vol.1" in *Calvin's Commentaries*, Vol 18, trans. Henry Beveridge (Grand Rapids, MI: Baker, 2003), 43.

6. Conclusion

There are two options here: the apostles got their theology wrong, or they got it right. Which is it?

Before you answer, let me remind you of two facts.

First, Jesus just spent forty days teaching them about the kingdom.

Second, the apostles' minds were supernaturally enabled to understand His teaching during that time.

So I put the question to you, what is more likely: that the apostles got the question exactly *wrong* (as Calvin thought), or that they got it exactly *right*?

I think they got it exactly right.

To counter Calvin, I think there are as many *truths* in their question as there are words. The apostles knew exactly what they were asking, and they were right to ask it. If that is right, you have to wonder: who is being carnal—the apostles or the commentators? As C. R. Stam noted,

> It is sometimes said that the apostles in asking this question, betrayed carnality and ignorance of the true nature of the kingdom which our Lord was to establish, but this charge is most unjust. The ignorance and carnality lie, not with the apostles but with their critics.[5]

---

[5] C. R. Stam, *The Book of Acts Dispensationally Considered* (Chicago, IL:

Let there be no mistake. The critics are wrong. Those who reject Premillennialism are wrong. Jesus taught that a literal kingdom for Israel was coming.

The apostles expected such a kingdom.

So do I.

So should you.

And if you do, the Biblical doctrine of election to service and reward will make far more sense to you.

Berean Bible Society, 1954): 1:33

The Difference Between Biblical Theology and Philosophical Theology

*Skepticism is the first step
on the road to philosophy.*
DENIS DIDEROT

WHERE'S THE PHILOSOPHY? As you come to the end of this book, no doubt some of you are asking that question.

When you picked up this book on election and predestination, you were expecting a work of philosophical theology. That is, you were expecting to read a book about time and eternity, possible worlds, modal logic, and how to reconcile free-will with God's providence. You might have been hoping for a novel solution to the endless debate between Determinists,[1] Thomists,[2] Molinists,[3] Boethians,[4] and Open Theists,[5] to name a few options.

But you didn't get that in this book.

Well, to be perfectly honest, I'm glad to disappoint you!

Don't misunderstand me. I think all of those questions are deeply fascinating (though not necessarily edifying or necessary for spiritual growth). I think they're worth spending *some* time thinking about. I have a whole bookshelf full of monographs on those questions. And maybe in another book I'll collect some of my thoughts about it.

But the simple fact is, I didn't raise those philosophical issues in this book *because they aren't directly part of the Biblical doctrine of election.*

In this book I am doing Biblical theology, not philosophical theology.

The difference between Biblical theology and philosophical theology is that Biblical theology

---

[1] Gordon H. Clark, *Predestination* (Philipsburg, NJ: P&R Publishing, 1987).

[2] Reginald Garrigou-Lagrange, *Predestination* (Charlotte, NC: Tan Books, 1939, 2013).

[3] William Lane Craig, *The Only Wise God: The Compatibility of Divine Foreknowledge and Human Freedom* (Grand Rapids, MI: Baker, 1987); John Correia, *Refreshing Grace* (Phoenix, AZ: Biblical Framework Press, 2012).

[4] Boethius, *The Consolation of Philosophy*, Book V.

[5] Clark Pinnock, "Divine Election as Corporate, Open, and Vocational." In *Perspectives on Election: Five Views*, ed. Chad Owen Brand (Nashville, TN: B&H Academic, 2006), 276-314.

sticks to what God has revealed, while philosophical theology often goes beyond the Biblical evidence, and more often than not, *doesn't consult the Biblical evidence at all.* The traditional views of election and predestination are a case in point. By and large, they have not grappled with the Biblical evidence.

As you and I discovered, the Biblical doctrine of election does not ask or answer the kinds of questions most often posed by systematic theologians ruminating about God's hidden will.

Instead, what the Bible has to say about election is down-to-earth and practical.

Biblical election is about the choices God makes about people, places, and things serving Him for reward.

The philosophical framework you use to explain *how* God can make those choices is a different issue from examining the Biblical basis *of the choices themselves.* If I ever write a book about God's providence, that's where I might raise and answer those kinds of questions.

But, to be perfectly honest, in these last few years I have been spiritually challenged to be a thoroughgoing Biblicist. That is, I've been challenged to humble myself and stay with the text— with what God has revealed—and not go beyond it. I've been learning to keep my mind chaste, as it were, and obedient. As a father of three young children, I know what it's like to have people asking me questions all day long. And I try to answer my kids' questions as much as I can. But sometimes I have to tell them, "You won't understand, so just trust me."

Instead of inventing answers to questions the Bible neither asks, nor answers, I find it better to humble myself and admit, "I don't know. The Bible does not say. But I trust God."

Scripture Index

Subject Index

Shawn Lazar is the Editor of *Grace in Focus* magazine and Director of Publications for Grace Evangelical Society.

Shawn was born and raised in Montreal, Canada. He has a BTh from McGill University and an MA from the Free University, Amsterdam.

He is the pastor of Gateway Baptist's Faith Fellowship. His previous book was *Beyond Doubt: How to Be Sure of Your Salvation.*

Shawn and his wife Abby, together with their three children, Daphne, Zane, and Scout, make their home in Denton, TX.

GRACE IN FOCUS is a free, bimonthly magazine about the gospel, assurance, and related issues.

You will read powerful testimonies, insightful Biblical studies, and encouraging practical lessons on living for Christ.

You will especially be presented with a clear saving message of faith alone, in Christ alone, for everlasting life that cannot be lost.

For your free U.S. subscription sign up at www.faithalone.org or send your name and address to P.O. Box 1308, Denton, TX 76202.